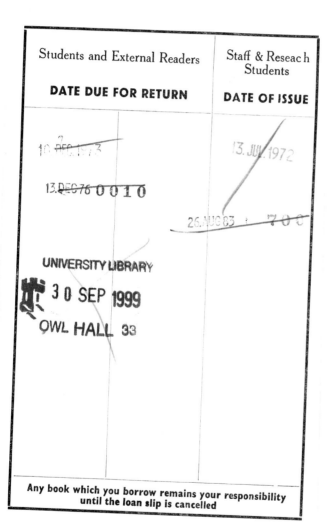

Wages in Practice and Theory

WAGES *in* PRACTICE *and* THEORY

McCormick and International Harvester
1860–1960

Robert Ozanne

THE UNIVERSITY OF WISCONSIN PRESS
Madison, Milwaukee, and London   1968

Published by the University of Wisconsin Press
Box 1379, Madison, Wisconsin 53701

The University of Wisconsin Press, Ltd.
27–29 Whitfield Street, London, W.1

Printed in the United States of America by
North Central Publishing Company, St. Paul, Minnesota

3

Library of Congress Catalog Card Number 68–19572

Preface

This book is part of a two-volume study of the evolution of industrial relations at the International Harvester Company and its principal predecessor, the McCormick Harvesting Machine Company. Both volumes center on the McCormick Works, that historic Chicago factory which produced agricultural machinery from 1847 through 1961. For many years this was the sole plant of the McCormick Harvesting Machine Company, and from 1902 to 1961 it was a principal plant of the International Harvester Company.

The first volume, *A Century of Labor-Management Relations*, is an account of the broad aspects of industrial relations history: the evolution of management policy toward labor, the growth of the personnel function, the nature of trade unionism. This, the second volume, is an economist's study of wage practice and theory. It is based on a detailed analysis of wage practice at the McCormick Works over the hundred years, 1860–1960. National data on wages, productivity, product and labor markets are extensively introduced for comparative purposes. Fully to understand the institutional setting of the wage practices described in this volume, the reader will find *A Century of Labor-Management Relations* most helpful.

The author and the public are greatly indebted to the McCormick family, for making available such complete and candid corporate and family records, and to the International Harvester Company, which expended great effort in locating additional information on wages and labor relations. Many officials of both the United Auto Workers and the International Harvester Company graciously submitted to prolonged hours of interviews in order to fill gaps in the written records. The International Union of Molders, Blacksmiths and Allied Workers kindly contributed its early records reaching back to 1863.

Mrs. Geeta Balakrishnan compiled most of the statistical data. Rajpal Rathee of the University Extension Division was in charge of the computation. Colleagues John Korbel (now of the University of New Hampshire), Arthur Goldberger, Harold Watts, and Arnold Zellner (now of the University of Chicago) of the Department of Economics gave statistical advice on the construction and treatment of the growth rates. The responsibility for their interpretation is solely mine. Financial support came from both the University of Wisconsin Graduate School and the University of Wisconsin Extension Division. The editors of the *Labor and Industrial Relations Review* and the *Review of Economics and Statistics* have given permission freely to use materials from articles by me which appeared in their journals.

Madison, Wisconsin   R. O.
December, 1967

Contents

Charts and Profiles

Tables

Wages in Practice and Theory

1

Introduction

The inflation of the post-World-War-II years sparked a new and critical look by economists at the factors responsible for wage movement. The continued rise of prices and wages through the business downturn of 1958 added a new dimension to the problem and provoked many new investigations. New efforts of governments to control wage movements under conditions of peacetime full employment over the past eight years in Europe and more recently in the United States give added impetus toward achieving better understanding of this complex problem. Lastly, the world-wide race to expedite economic growth of under-developed countries has led to a closer examination of the early economic development of the developed countries, including their wage behavior.

Despite these recent opportunities to study wage behavior under differing economic conditions, as of 1967 the economists were badly split as to the appropriate weight to be attached to the various factors determining wages. A corollary of this is their inability to reach agreement on appropriate wage policies in the face of inflation.

Today's wage theorist is sadly handicapped by the lack of elementary data once he gets back before the 1930's. The National Bureau of Economic Research has recognized this by encouraging several studies for the collection of early wage data.[1] These excellent compilations, building on the earlier work of Douglas [2] and others, have concentrated on getting a composite picture of average hourly earnings in manufacturing over at least the last one hundred years.

3

The primary shortcoming of the NBER studies is that their composite nature prohibits much analysis aimed at differentiating the various factors associated with wage movement. Thus Rees, skillfully working backward from the annual census totals of payrolls, average number of employees, and days and hours worked for the period 1890–1914, arrives at annual average rates of hourly earnings which conceal most causal clues. From annual census data, a 12 per cent wage increase in December cannot be differentiated from a 1 per cent increase in the preceding January. The secrecy and timing of census data prevent following the wage policy of a firm from year to year and week to week. A depression-induced wage cut of 15 per cent in December followed by February strikes restoring the cut would barely register in the bland census data and would greatly underestimate the magnitude of wage movement. The census data are likewise silent on employee turnover and its causes, on the impact of trade unionism on corporate wage policy, on the wage impact of political pressures, and on monopsonistic firm practices in the purchase of labor.

To learn more about the wage-decision-making process it is important to study the locus of wage decision making — the firm. This study, therefore, focuses first on the wage patterns and wage decisions of one firm over the period 1858–1960. Wage data from a single plant, the McCormick Works, have been assembled for the entire period and intensively analyzed. For comparative purposes, similar precise data have been assembled for two additional competing agricultural implement plants, one from 1882 to 1902 and the other from 1882 to 1896. Hence, this is a study of comparative wage behavior both "money" and "real" over the period roughly 1850–1860, rather than the more common inter-industry study covering only very recent time periods.

Secondly, beginning with Chapter 4 this study assembles for the entire hundred-year period, and compares with the McCormick Works wage movement the more traditional macro-wage data — average hourly earnings for U.S. manufacturing. This parallel comparison of both types of data permits important though tentative implications for general wage theory.

In such a study of such relatively small segments of the labor force, it is not possible to reach conclusions on trends of income shares. No data are presented to indicate what other group gained when real wage growth was low nor who lost when real wage growth was high.

Though burned to the ground by the famous Chicago fire of 1871 and rebuilt in a new location, the McCormick Works at its closing in 1961 had produced grain harvesting machinery for 112 continuous years. Wage data for this study were taken directly from the original payroll books of the plant for the periods 1848–1849 and 1858–1914 (the payroll books, though not the payroll totals, for 1850–1857 have been lost). McCormick Works wage averages from 1915 through 1960 have been supplied by the International Harvester Company. Payroll books through 1940 have been used for special studies of individual departments.

Wage data of this precise nature enable wage changes to be pinpointed to the exact day of the change. The unique combination of correspondence of top company officials and payroll data proved to be invaluable in throwing light on the causes for wage movements. The ability to trace wage policy over a hundred-year period gives an unparalleled opportunity to observe the evolution of wage practices and to check theoretical hypotheses under widely varying conditions — wars, prosperity, depression, labor market shortages and surpluses, before and after changes in immigration laws, in the presence and absence of trade unionism.

Chart 1 shows wage changes at the McCormick Works and for U.S. manufacturing, varying not only from depression to prosperity, from wartime to peacetime, but also varying widely in differing periods of peacetime prosperity. Moreover the wage growth rates indicated by the slope of the lines on Chart 1 do not appear generally to vary annually but frequently continue at similar rates for periods up to 8 or 10 years. Strikes, indicated by asterisks, appear generally to coincide with periods of rapid wage changes, more often up than down. The close coincidence of McCormick Works and U.S. manufacturing wages since 1900 is significant and like the impact of strikes and unionism will be further explored. The top line, depicting real wages for the McCormick Works, does not change the conclusion regarding the varying rates of wage change, though it does deflate the high rate of money wage changes in wartime.

The use of the real wage data such as in Chart 1 is necessarily based on a long-run cost-of-living index. There are certain inherent shortcomings in such an index. However, in the succeeding chapters the extensive use of rates of change in real wage growth rates, especially

Chart 1. Average Hourly Earnings, 1849, 1858–1960, McCormick Works and U.S. Manufacturi

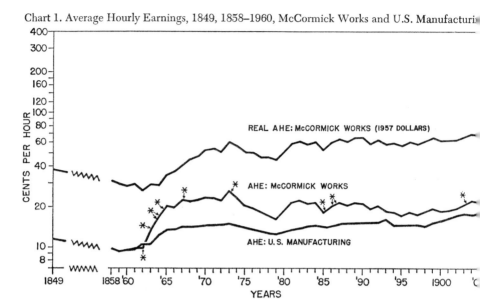

Asterisks and arrows along the McCormick wage line indicate strikes.

Sources: See Appendix A for data and all sources except those for strike dates, which are fr
correspondence in the McCormick Collection, from Payroll Books of the McCormick Harvest

for the short-term periods of 5 to 13 years, are reasonably free from such shortcomings.

Prior to 1900 the national wage patterns and the McCormick wage patterns diverge widely at times (Chart 1). The McCormick wages were more volatile, rising more during the Civil War and the prosperity of 1870–1873 and falling more during the long depression of the seventies. Similarly, in the eighties the McCormick wages rose more in the early eighties and fell precipitously in the depression of 1884–1885. In the national averages this depression is scarcely a ripple. From the eighties until 1902 the differential between McCormick wages and the national average declined substantially, due to an actual decline in McCormick wages. Beginning with the turn of the century and particularly with World War I, the national wage pattern, while noticeable in the earlier years, is clearly dominant in the McCormick wage trend.

A. W. Philips studied British wage growth rates[3] during almost the same years as this study. Philips' main concern was to learn whether money wages rose more rapidly during periods of labor shortage than in periods of labor surplus. As would be expected, he found that money

d Real AHE, McCormick Works

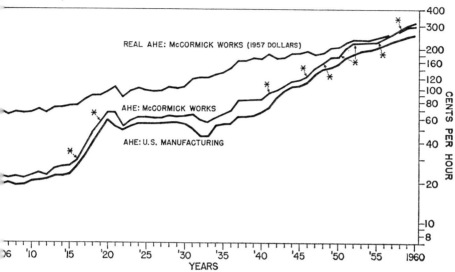

REAL AHE: McCORMICK WORKS (1957 DOLLARS)

AHE: McCORMICK WORKS

AHE: U.S. MANUFACTURING

CENTS PER HOUR

400
300
200
160
120
100
80
60
40
20
10
8

'06 '10 '15 '20 '25 '30 '35 '40 '45 '50 '55 1960
YEARS

achine Co., from the Files of the National Defense Mediation Board, which are in the National
chives, Washington, and from Robert B. McKersie, "Structural Factors and Negotiations in
e I-H Co.," in Arnold R. Webber, ed., *The Structure of Collective Bargaining* (Glencoe, Ill.:
e Free Press, 1961), p. 280.

wages rose more rapidly during prosperity and especially during wartime. (Chart 1 indicates the same finding for the McCormick works
and for U.S. manufacturing.) Philips noted that there were certain
minor deviations from market demand behavior. Specifically, he referred
to the influence of combinations of employers, to trade union pressures,
and to extreme rises in the price of imports.[4]

This study takes for granted the findings of the Philips study — that
wages rise more rapidly in prosperity and in wartime than in depressions — and focuses on the causes of the phenomenon of differing rates
of wage change during periods of peacetime prosperity over the last
100 years. No effort is made to give numerical weight to the varied
causes of wage movements in different periods since the accuracy of
necessary data does not go back much before 1930. Nor is any formula
proposed which might explain the exact magnitude of wage rate changes
in the recent past nor predict the future.

For this analysis, major periods of prosperity have been set forth in
Table 1, which also includes for perspective the behavior of wages
in wartime and depressions.

TABLE 1

Wage Growth Rates in Prosperity, Depressions, Wars — U.S. Manufacturing and the McCormick Works

	Annual percentage rates of growth in AHE production workers U.S. manufacturing		Annual percentage rates of growth in AHE production workers McCormick Works	
	Money AHE (1)	Real AHE (2)	Money AHE (3)	Real AHE (4)
PEACETIME PROSPERITY				
1865–1873	1.2[a]	5.0	2.4	6.8
1880–1887	1.6	3.0	0.0	1.4
1887–1893	1.0	1.8	−2.0	−1.2
1900–1903	4.1	2.5	4.4[b]	2.8
1905–1913	2.2	1.0	1.5	0.4
1923–1929	1.1	1.1	0.9	0.9
1947–1960	5.3	3.3	5.8	3.6
Seven Prosperity Periods average (51 yrs.)	2.6	2.7	2.2	2.4
MAJOR DEPRESSIONS				
1873–1879	−2.9	0.4	−7.5	−4.8
1893–1898	−1.5	0.0	−0.6	0.9
1920–1922	−8.2	0.6	−12.1	−3.7
1929–1933	−6.8	0.6	−2.4	5.7
Four Major Depressions average (17 yrs.)	−4.0	.35	−4.8	− .5
MAJOR WARS				
1861–1865	8.2	−7.4	22.2	4.7
1914–1920	18.4	4.6	18.7	4.8
1940–1946	9.3	3.7	6.7	1.7
Three Major Wars average (16 yrs.)	12.4	1.3	15.1	3.6
1860–1960	3.1	2.2	2.9	2.0

[a] The concept used in the computations of the growth rates is that of a least squares line drawn through each annual observation. The rate computed approximates a constant annual percentage increase. This method takes the place of the more commonly used average annual percentage rates of change (simple compound interest formula) calculated from only the beginning and ending observations. Growth rates are used throughout except in a few cases where data are combined with information from other sources using the simple compound interest formula.

Whether or not the different rates for different periods represent significant

In this study both the "money" and "real" wage concepts are employed at appropriate times. For day-to-day and month-to-month wage changes, the "money" wage is essential. For meaningful comparisons over more than a few months, the "real" wage concept is essential.

As might be expected, the average rate of wage increase of prosperity periods substantially exceeds that of depressions. The wage behavior of each war has its own explanation depending on the intensity of the war and the nature of government controls. These differences, particularly the difference in McCormick and U.S. manufacturing wage behavior in the Civil War, are discussed in Chapter 2.

The surprising finding of Table 1 is the wide variation in wage behavior during prosperity periods. In U.S. manufacturing, rates of real wage change range from an average of 5 per cent per year for the 1865–1873 period to approximately 1 per cent in the 1905–1913 and the 1923–1929 periods. In the McCormick Works the rate of real wage change range was even greater, from 6.8 per cent in 1865–1873 to −1.2 per cent from 1887 to 1893. The real wage increase rate of 3.6 per cent for the recent 1947–1960 period is perhaps more significant than the one of 1865–1873, since this latest prosperity occurred in a somewhat inflationary period, whereas the 1865–1873 prosperity was in deflationary times and because the latter was a much longer period.

The purpose of studying wage behavior in prosperity periods is to eliminate insofar as possible the major cyclical influences and thus make easier the identification of those wage-affecting factors other than level of product and labor market demand.

The other factors which are examined in this study as possible wage-

differences is discussed briefly after Table 2 of this chapter and in detail in Chapter 3 in connection with the data of Table 9.

[b] (3) goes as far as January, 1904, to reflect the wage raise given in accordance with the union agreement of May, 1903.

Sources: (1), (2), 1858–1958, Clarence D. Long, "The Illusion of Wage Rigidity," *Review of Economics and Statistics*, 42, No. 2, Part 1 (May, 1960): 150–51; 1959–1960, *Economic Report of the President*, 1963. Fringe Benefits have been added to (1), (2) for the years 1939–1958 from computations by Albert Rees, *New Measures of Wage-Earner Compensation in Manufacturing, 1914–57*, Occasional Paper 75 (Princeton, N.J.: National Bureau of Economic Research, Inc., 1960), pp. 3–4, Table 1, and for 1958–1960 from *Economic Report of the President*, 1962, p. 177, Table 22.

(3), (4), 1860–1914, McCormick Payroll Record, McCormick Collection; 1915–1960, I.H.Co. records, Chicago. Fringe benefits have also been added to (3), 1939–1960, on the assumption that they constituted the same per cent of McCormick Works wages as of manufacturing wages.

determining factors are trade unionism (Chapter 4), productivity (Chapter 6), and the degree of concentration in the product market (Chapter 7).

The classification of periods of prosperity and depression — (1) in Table 1 — is of necessity a somewhat loose one. All periods of "prosperity" include some recession years, such as 1867, 1884, 1908, 1927, 1949, 1954, and 1958. Periods of prolonged depression, however, have been avoided — 1873–1879, 1893–1898, 1921–1922, 1929–1933. Some very brief prosperity periods, 1919–1920, 1936–1937 and 1940–1941, were omitted because no meaningful wage growth rate could be established in such short periods. The 1919–1920 period was added to the World War I period.

In the selection of prosperity periods, I was guided by the business cycle reference chart of the National Bureau of Economic Research.[5] All of the ending dates are from this source. I deliberately skipped the first year of the upturn in each cycle in order better to measure wage behavior during prosperity.

The four long depressions listed in Table 1 are of little significance in this study. Obviously their rates of real wage increase are below those of prosperity periods. The lag in wage cuts in depressions in recent years is studied in Chapter 4.

A feature of this wage study is its use of time periods rather than of inter-industry comparisons. This is done because the wage causal variables appear to be more associated with time periods than with industries. Table 2 gives a measure of the relative importance of inter-time period versus inter-industry wage variations based on two equal length periods of prosperity, 1923–1929 and 1953–1959.

The emphatic conclusion from Table 2 is that whatever factors caused wage variation in the periods 1923–1929 and 1953–1959 affected all the industries of Table 2 substantially alike. There were minor relative shifts amongst industries but they were dwarfed by the wage growth rate explosion which hit them all sometime between 1929 and 1953.

An analysis of variance was computed comparing the variance between the two time periods with the variance among the industries. The F ratio showed that the variance between the time periods was 32.5 times the variance among industries. This computed value of 32.5 far exceeds the critical value at the 1 per cent significance level of 8.86 shown in the F Table for the appropriate degrees of freedom.

This major phenomenon of average rate of wage change varying

TABLE 2

Changes in Rank of Selected Industries According to Rate of Growth in
Real Wages Between 1923–1929 and 1953–1959

Industry	1923–1929		1953–1959	
	Ranked by rate of growth (1)	Annual percentage rates of growth, real AHE (2)	Ranked by rate of growth (3)	Annual percentage rates of growth, real AHE (4)
Chemicals	1	1.89	3	3.75
Iron and Steel	2	1.15	1	5.22
Meat Packing	3	1.12	2	4.93
McCormick Works[a]	4	0.93	4	3.63
Paper	5	0.84	5	3.58
Rubber	6	0.76	7	3.02
Machinery	7	0.69	6	3.08
Textiles	8	0.43	8	1.33
Eight Industry Average Growth Rates		0.98		3.57

[a] Used as a proxy for agricultural implements except tractors.

Sources: (2), 1923–1929 (all industries except McCormick), National Industrial Conference Board, *The Economic Almanac, 1951–1952* (New York: NICB, 1951), p. 270; McCormick 1923–1929, I.H.Co. Records, Chicago.

(4), 1953–1959 (all industries except McCormick), U. S. Dept. of Commerce, Office of Business Economics, *Business Statistics* (Washington, D.C.: GPO, 1961); U. S. Dept. of Labor Statistics, *Employment and Earning Statistics for the United States, 1909–1960* (Washington, D.C.: GPO, 1961); McCormick Works Average 1953–1959; I.H.Co. Records, Chicago.

significantly over time is missed by the current emphasis on interindustry studies of both the cross-sectional (in the same year) and the over-time types. The major causal factors behind wage movements are apparently rarely confined to one industry but spill over and diffuse among many industries. There are good theoretical grounds for supposing that the wage effects of labor market conditions and trade unionism spread rapidly from firm to firm and industry to industry.

These movements would be only partially observable by inter-industry studies. Eckstein and Wilson in an inter-industry study covering 1948–1960 could not isolate the effects of unionism despite the use of elaborate statistical techniques: "Because of spillovers, any wage increases caused by unionization would permeate much of the wage structure of other industries. . . ."[6]

This phenomenon of the rate of change of average hourly earnings of broadly differing industries varying primarily by time period rather than by industry was also noted by Kendrick.[7] Kendrick compiled percentage changes in average hourly earnings by rank for 33 industries from 1899 to 1953 and for six subperiods. For the six subperiods the coefficient of variation of industry groups relative to the mean group change was only .09, which was considerably below the coefficient of variation of percentage changes in productivity. He also found that serial correlation of the industry group ranks with respect to average hourly earnings in each subperiod with the industry group ranks in the previous subperiod yielded coefficients above +.9 in all subperiods after 1909.[8]

Time period comparisons limited to relatively recent periods are by no means new. Albert Rees made such a study comparing wage movements in the inflations of the World War I and World War II periods.[9] This writer made use of wage comparison over time by comparing wage behavior in a non-union period, 1923–1929, and a union period, 1947–1957.[10] This study assembles data on wage movements and possible causal factors as far back as 1858.

This detailed study of the McCormick wages might be expected to reveal not only why both "money" and "real" McCormick wages departed from national trends at some points, but more ambitiously, information on the causes of the national trends. Though no one case study such as this can presume to be representative of American manufacturing generally, the conclusions on wage theory which it yields will be important hypotheses for further testing with wage studies of other companies.

In order carefully to study the nature and timing of McCormick wage changes, McCormick Works wage data have been put on a series of twelve period chronology charts called profiles. These profiles permit breaking down the inexactness of the typical wage data based on annual averages. On these profiles are changes in rates of pay whenever they occurred in a given year, e.g., a 25 per cent increase in May and a 25 per cent cut in September of the same year.

The analysis accompanying each profile attempts to interpret the wage movements by bringing to bear on each major wage movement much of the pertinent information from the correspondence of McCormick and Harvester executives, union records, newspaper accounts, and miscellaneous other sources. Here, various causes of wage movement, market demand for labor, costs of living, union activity, productivity, the nature of the product market and government action are analyzed.

Following the analysis of the twelve wage periods Chapter 3 continues the same type of wage chronologies as Chapter 2, but adds comparative data for two other Chicago area agricultural implement firms. This comparative company wage data includes only the years from about 1882 to 1902 since in that year all firms became part of the International Harvester Company.

In successive chapters the impacts on money and real wages of such factors as trade unionism, market demand for labor, productivity, and the nature of the product market are statistically analyzed. A special section, Appendix D, covers the changing occupational differential from 1860 to 1960.

2

Wage Profiles

This chapter[1] contains twelve period chronology profiles as follows: 1849–1861, 1861–1866, 1866–1873, 1873–1879, 1879–1887, 1887–1897, 1897–1916, 1916–1920, 1920–1932, 1932–1940, 1940–1949, 1949–1960. The break points are not significant: their function is to pinpoint exact changes in rates of pay. The accompanying analyses attempt to throw light on the causes of the wage changes by use of such data as correspondence of company executives, strikes, union records, newspaper accounts, turnover data, and pertinent government policies.

The term "profile" is used here instead of "chart" merely to indicate more frequent observations of wage data; in the charts only annual observations are recorded, whereas the profiles record all significant wage changes whenever they occurred. The average hourly earnings line on these same profiles merely connects annual observations. Each profile contains the following information:

a. The plant average wage. These are the same figures as are on Chart 1 for 1849 and 1858–1914. This average is for the first week in April[2] and it is the combined average hourly earnings of the day and piece rate workers minus supervisors. From 1915 to 1924 it is the yearly average. From 1941 to 1960 the average excludes overtime. The plant average wage in the profiles does not include estimates of fringe benefits, thus differing slightly from the data of Chart 1 and the growth rate tables for the period 1939–1960.

b. The common labor chronology. This shows exact date of changes, and does not include fringe benefits. It is accurate to the month.

c. The skilled day rate chronology. From 1858 through 1888, this is an average of hourly rates of the upper sextile of day rate workers. Beginning with 1888, the average of the pattern shop craftsmen replaces the upper sextile. This does not include fringe benefits. Significant wage changes are shown whenever they occurred; the chronology is accurate to the month. Individual wage changes are not shown, but whenever a group of workers, such as even a sub-group within a department was raised, the change in the average is indicated. Discontinuities in the upper sextile rates are due to changes in the averages caused by a change in the skill mix without a change in individual rates of pay.

d. McCormick Works employment as of each April. This is indicated at the bottom of the profiles, measured by a separate scale on the right.

e. The strikes of the McCormick Works plus one strike (1903) of the company's Deering Works, whose contract settlement covered the McCormick Works. These are indicated by asterisks.

The years 1849 and 1858–1861, covered in Profile 1, are the best examples in the company's long wage history of non-union wage behavior. The distinguishing features of this period are the general wage decline, 1849–1859, and the unique seasonal wage movements, 1858–1861.

There are three probable causes of the decline: immigration, work simplification, and the recession of 1858. Immigration tripled in the early 1850's; this no doubt made a real change in the labor supply situation. Although 1849 was the first full year of reaper manufacturing by the McCormicks, ten years later great strides must have been made in simplification and division of work so that a higher proportion of unskilled workmen could be used. For example, in 1849 the modal pay rate was 12.5 cents per hour, a skilled or semi-skilled rate. In 1859 the modal rate was 6.2 cents per hour, the common labor rate. A third cause of the wage decline was apparently the recession of 1858. Seasonal wage cuts were made in September, 1858, but again in November common labor was cut back to a new low for this period, from 7.5 cents per hour to 6.2 cents. This must have reflected an eased labor supply condition in the community, because employment increased at McCormick Harvesting Machine Company from 1858 to 1859 at the same time that wage rates were being cut.

The payroll books for the 1850–1857 period have been lost. The

Profile 1. Classical Wage Movements: 1849–1861

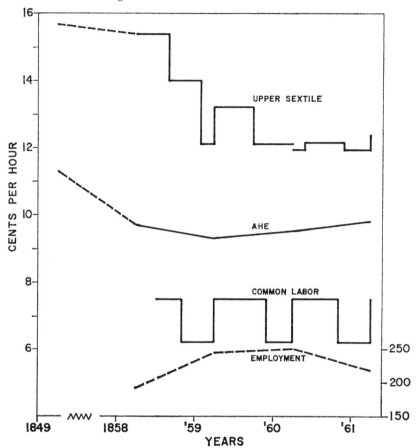

Includes average hourly day rates for skilled labor, AHE for the entire plant, the rate for common labor, and plant-wide employment, 1849, 1858–1861, McCormick Works.

Source: McCormick Works payroll books, in the McCormick Collection.

firm's ledgers reveal only total labor cost. Table 3 shows some variations in labor cost per machine, but gives almost no clues as to wage rates. The increased proportion of labor cost in 1854 is due to the fact that the company bought a foundry; molders wages raised the proportion of labor cost temporarily.

The data in Table 3 imply quite variable wage rates from 1852 to 1853. The declining unit labor cost after 1854 may well have occurred due to greater efficiency rather than to wage cuts. Profile 1 indicates that wage rates in 1859 were slightly below the 1858 level, yet labor costs per machine rose slightly due to a drop in the number of machines produced.

The second distinguishing feature of this period is the seasonal movement of wages. The agricultural implement business was seasonal. If a good year was anticipated, production of reapers was stepped up in January, rising to a peak in June and July, after which production

TABLE 3

Reapers Manufactured, Machine Manufacturing Costs, Machine Labor Costs, and Wages as a Per Cent of Manufacturing Cost, 1851–1859, C. H. McCormick and Bros.

Year ending	Reaping machines manufactured	Manufacturing cost per machine	Labor cost per machine	Wages as a per cent of manufacturing cost
8/30/1851	1004	$36.15	$ 9.54	26.3
8/28/52	1011	38.28	11.45	29.9
8/27/53	1101	56.92	17.00	29.8
8/26/54[a]	1558	56.07	22.22	39.6
8/25/55	2534	54.71	16.50	30.0
8/30/56	4095	47.90	13.16	27.4
8/29/57	4091	50.27	14.74	29.3
8/28/58	4563	42.57	12.06	28.3
8/29/59	4119	46.58	12.74	27.3

[a] In this year the company added a grey iron foundry to the works.

Source: Data for this chart are from an unpublished University of Wisconsin Ph.D. thesis in progress by John Lehman. Data are based on Journals and Day Books, McCormick and Bros.

tapered off and employment declined. Skilled men worked the year round, but common laborers were hired for the season. Spring wage increases at McCormick's were selective. There was no such thing as a general wage increase, but in a good year, over a three-week period in March and April 70 per cent of the workers received increases. In this period, flat increases of 1.25 cents per hour were most common – given to both the 6.2 cent per hour laborer and the 11.2 cent skilled worker. The purpose of this spring wage increase was no doubt to lessen the competition for labor of the building construction industry, which worked only in the summer months. Fall wage cuts came when cold weather stopped building construction; an early company brochure told of the attractiveness of winter work in a heated factory.

The work day throughout the period was ten hours per day from

1849 to 1916, with two temporary periods of shorter work days in 1886 and 1903–1904. Workers were paid weekly. Overtime was paid to all day-rate workers at straight-time rates until World War I, with the exception of 1903–1904.

The Civil War Inflation, 1861–1866

The Civil War inflation got off to a slow start. After Fort Sumter came a short business recession. The fall of 1861 saw the usual seasonal wage cuts at McCormick's. At first glance, 1862–1864 looks like a classic period of inflation, but wage Profile 2 shows two significant changes over the profile for the previous (1849–1861) period. The spring season of 1862 saw two rounds of wage increases instead of one, and, for the first time, in the fall of 1862, there was a wage increase instead of the traditional post-season cuts. This new pattern lasted for the rest of the war.

Contrary to expectations, Chart 1 shows that, except for a possible lag in early 1862, McCormick wages rose a bit faster than prices. McCormick workers had small real wage gains right through the fast moving Civil War inflation. Thus the common assumption that during inflations wages lag behind prices was not true at McCormick's in the Civil War inflation.

What were the causes of this Civil War wage pattern? The basic upward movement was due to the acute labor shortage resulting from the Civil War draft and the economic expansion caused by government war orders financed by such inflationary fiscal policies as the issuance of greenbacks. Average Civil War wages in U.S. manufacturing, as tabulated by Long, did lag substantially behind prices. Why then did wages at the McCormick Harvesting Machine Company keep abreast of inflation?

The inflation had hardly begun before militant unions arose. The payroll books reveal frequent work stoppages, particularly in the foundry, and newspaper and company correspondence chronicle a running labor-management struggle. As early as September 28, 1862, William McCormick, in a report to his brother Cyrus, refers to the harassment of "strikes of foundrymen, and general demands for advanced wages." Indeed the molders at McCormick's conducted at least six strikes between 1862 and 1865. Their wages responded emphatically, more than keeping pace with the cost-of-living changes. The modal molder at McCormick's made 17 cents per hour in April, 1863; 30 cents in 1864; and 40 cents in 1865.

Wage theorists recently have speculated that in intense inflationary periods employers would raise wages more rapidly without unions than with them since union contracts would stabilize wages for at least the contract period. The Civil War experience of the McCormick Harvesting Machine Company implies that the unions of that day made use

file 2. The Civil War Inflation: 1861–1866

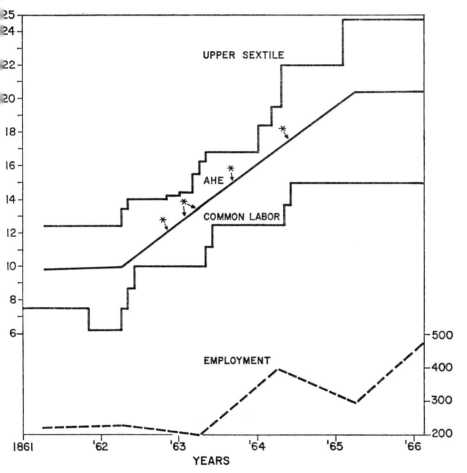

ludes average hourly day rates for skilled labor, AHE for the entire plant, the rate for com-
n labor, and plant-wide employment, 1861–1866, McCormick Works. Asterisks and arrows
icate strikes.

irce: McCormick Works payroll books, in the McCormick Collection.

of the supposed advantages of both union and non-union behavior. The unions faced by the McCormick Company made their demands several times a year, backing them up with strikes whenever necessary. The agreements were oral and had no set duration. There can be no doubt after reading the correspondence of the McCormick brothers that vigorous union activity forced the company to raise wages both higher and more often than even the tight Civil War labor markets called for. Employers such as the McCormicks retaliated by making agreements with other firms to hold down wages.

TABLE 4

Average Hourly Earnings, U.S. Manufacturing and McCormick (Day Rate), 1861–1865

Year	U.S. AHE in manufacturing (1)	McCormick AHE as of the first week in April (2)
1861	9.7¢	9.8¢
1862	10.6	9.9
1863	10.7	13.5
1864	12.2	17.0
1865	13.4	20.4

Sources: (1) Clarence D. Long, "The Illusion of Wage Rigidity," *Review of Economics and Statistics*, 42, No. 2, Part 1 (May, 1960), pp. 150–51.
(2) McCormick Works payroll books, in the McCormick Collection.

The U.S. manufacturing averages compiled by Long (see Chart 1) give a picture of national Civil War wage behavior somewhat different from the one at McCormick's. Table 4 details the contrast.

The U.S. averages imply that the McCormick wage movements were atypical of the Civil War period, particularly from 1862 to 1863, when national averages were stable. Long's national wage average for manufacturing, when compared with cost-of-living changes, shows a wage lag during the Civil War inflation, with real income falling 21 per cent from 1861 to 1865, whereas the McCormick workers increased their real income 19 per cent during the same period.

Further comparison of the McCormick plant data and the Long national averages reveals strikingly the need for data of the McCormick type to supplement national averages. The detailed national Aldrich data,[3] source of the Long averages, show 1862–1863 to be a period of rapid wage movement, often upward as at McCormick's, but also downward in isolated manufacturing towns or where lack of cotton depressed northern textile mills. Yet the national averages for 1862 and 1863, as in Table 1, imply a period of wage stability.

Assuming that Long's data are adequately weighted by industry and occupation, the stable average which he found for 1862–1863, in the face of widely divergent wage trends in different firms and industries, indicates a high degree of labor immobility. The causes of such immobility may have been the isolation of manufacturing villages and the relatively poor transportation and communication of that era. It is highly probable that it was the vigorous union activity at McCormick's which kept wages abreast of inflation during the Civil War. For the rest of manufacturing, some of the wage lag can be assessed against the unemployment in the textile industry and some against the presumed lesser degree of unionism in remote manufacturing towns. The *Journal of the Molders' Union* gives statistics of wage gains made during the Civil War which imply that union activity in Chicago was not atypical of that in many of the larger cities.

In view of the high degree of union activity at McCormick's during the Civil War, which Molders' Union records indicate was duplicated in other cities, it is possible that United States industrial history may be devoid of any inflationary period which will demonstrate on a broad scale pure non-union behavior.

Rising Wages, Falling Prices, 1866–1873

In 1866 there was a return to the pre-Civil War pattern of spring raises and fall cuts with no noticeable rise in the mean wage for the first time since 1861. This return to the seasonal wage pattern of pre-Civil war days suggests that the wartime labor shortage was over.

Early May, 1867, shows something new: the McCormick payroll books reveal that, for the first time in the company's history, a general wage increase was given. Moreover, it was given in the middle of the payroll week. The amount of the increase was a straight 10 per cent for all. Earlier increases had been either 12.5 cents or 25 cents per ten-hour day. The cause of this new wage pattern was a plant-wide strike for the eight-hour day, indicating the first try at industrial unionism.

It is significant that, in contrast to the Civil War strikes, this strike took place during the recession of 1867 when Chicago had a surplus of workers,[4] employment at the McCormick plant was declining, and the cost of living was dropping. While the wage increases of the Civil War period were magnified by union activity, the more important cause was the war-created shortage of labor. Since this 1867 wage increase took place in a recession, union activity appears in this case to have been the dominant cause. In the fall of 1867, after the season's machines had been completed, the McCormick Company rescinded the 10 per cent wage increase. In this stable period, lack of long-term con-

Profile 3. Rising Wages, Falling Prices: 1866–1873

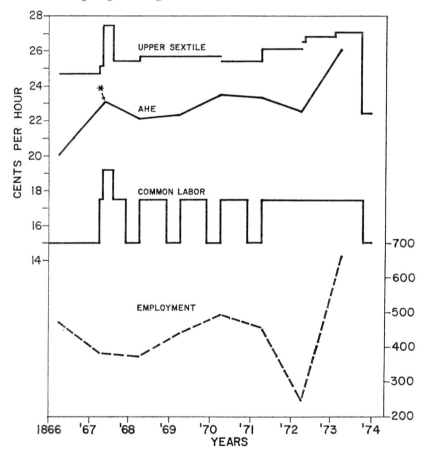

Includes average hourly day rate for skilled labor (discontinuities due to a change in the skill mix, not to a change in wage rates), AHE for the entire plant, the rate for common labor, and plant-wide employment, 1866–1874, McCormick Works. Average hourly earnings for 1867 are as of June 1 instead of April 1 to reflect the effect of the May Day strike. Asterisk and arrow indicate a strike.

Source: McCormick Works payroll books, in the McCormick Collection.

tracts hurt the unions. Workers and employers still continued to think of wage rates in terms of "the season."

The next wage peak at McCormick's was during 1871–1873. This coincides with a national peak in trade union activity, with which union activity in Chicago kept pace. Iron Molders' Local 23 was particularly busy. Its membership list reached 545 in 1872[5] and probably rose considerably in 1873 when the new McCormick foundry and the new Malleable Iron Company foundry opened.

Money wages of McCormick workers rose from an average of 20.4 cents per hour in 1865 to 26.1 cents in 1873. Real wages rose 74.2 per cent, or 6.8 per cent per year, in this eight-year period. If the period is stretched backward to include 1864, the time when the cost of living began its decline, the real wage rise for the nine-year period is substantially higher.

Rising wages and falling prices were thus a reality during this entire period. Like the Civil War period, the 1870–1873 wage peak at McCormick's was due to a combination of market demand and union pressure, with market demand playing a lesser role than in wartime.

The great Chicago fire of October, 1871, destroyed the McCormick Works. The firm operated for a short time thereafter with a much reduced payroll, retaining a high proportion of the skilled workers and laying off many unskilled. In 1873 employment returned to normal. The 1872–1873 wage peak proved to be the peak for almost half a century to come as the long recession of the seventies, the continued decline in consumer prices, the employer offensive against unions of the middle and late eighties, and continued immigration combined to act as a long-run depressant on wages.

The Long Depression, 1873–1879

In the long depression of the seventies, the McCormick Harvesting Machine Company showed itself adept at quickly adjusting labor cost to changing market conditions. By August 4, 1873, the company saw that it would have unsold machines on hand and instructed its agents to make concessions to unload them.[6] In mid-August the firm shut down the foundry for a month, and made drastic cuts in foundry day rates and piece rates when it reopened in September. The molders refused to work at the reduced rates and in turn went out on strike for a month. In late October the molders, after two months without work, accepted a wage cut. There appears to have been a compromise on piece rates.

The company followed up its victory over the molders by cutting wages in the entire plant except for the lowest paid workers. The wage cuts in the foundry actually preceded the financial panic which hit the banking system in mid-September, 1873. At the same time it was cutting wages, the company was ordering raw materials for a record production of ten thousand machines for the 1874 season.[7]

Profile 4. The Long Depression: 1873–1879

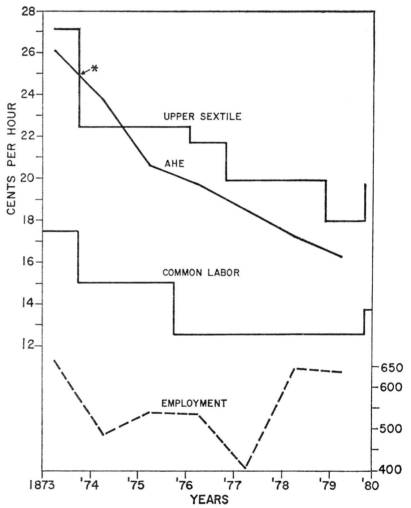

Includes average hourly day rates for skilled labor, AHE for the entire plant, the rate for common labor, and plant-wide employment, 1873–1879, McCormick Works. Asterisk and arrow indicate a strike.

Source: McCormick Works payroll books, in the McCormick Collection.

Note in Profile 4 how for the year 1874 total AHE exceeded even the average of the upper sextile of day rates. Piece-rate earnings were always higher than day-rate earnings, but in this year of wage reductions the piece workers could by extra effort win back a part of their cuts.

As Profile 4 shows, there were four successive wage cuts for skilled labor from 1873 through 1878, but only two for the unskilled. The records do not reveal the cause for the greater and more frequent wage cuts of the skilled workers. I can only speculate that it was a management maneuver designed to minimize worker suffering and labor troubles. Cutting the lowest paid workers might result in riots. Furthermore, timing the cuts so that not all workers were cut at once minimized the likelihood of united strike action. Mean day-rate wages fell 32 per cent from 1872 to 1879. A favorite time for wage cuts was the fall reopening after a lay-off: workers just rescued from unemployment were not prone to striking and with winter coming on were thankful for a job regardless of the wage. The wage cuts in this period exceeded the cost-of-living decline so that the workers suffered real wage cuts as well as the loss of income through fewer weeks of work.

Table 5 permits a comparison of employment[8] and net profit figures

TABLE 5

Employment and Profits, McCormick Harvesting Machine Company, 1871–1879

Year	Total factory employment first week in April (1)	Net profits McCormick Harvesting Machine Company (2)
1871	464	$358,894
1873	667	—[a]
1874	477	287,000
1875	547	630,000
1876	539	—[a]
1877	393	325,000
1878	656	618,000
1879	640	722,326

[a]Not available

Sources: (1), McCormick Works payroll books, in the McCormick Collection.

(2), letter, C. A. Spring to C.H.McC., Sept. 1, 1871, CHMcC I Papers; letter, Frank H. Mathews to C.H.McC., Sept. 22, 1874, CHMcC I Papers; letter, Frank H. Mathews to C.H.McC., Oct. 4, 1875, CHMcC I Papers; William T. Hutchinson, *Cyrus Hall McCormick*, 2 vols. (New York: D. Appleton-Century Co., 1935), II: 607, *n.* 117 (for 1877 and 1878); ibid., p. 690, *n.* 10 (for 1879).

during the long recession which began in the fall of 1873 and lasted till 1879. Wage cuts were not the result of any severe financial pressures, but rather the result of normal and systematic efforts to cut all costs of production in line with market conditions during the depression. Manufacturing cost per machine dropped from $107.45 in 1873 to $38.25 in 1879.[9] Labor cost in 1879 was 39 per cent of manufacturing cost.

Though nationally the new trade unions of the sixties fell apart with the onset of the long depression in 1873, this was not so at McCormick's. Comparison of union records [10] and McCormick payrolls indicate that many of the McCormick molders were union members throughout the long depression. Although the company victory in the October, 1873, strike established the company's ability to cut wages, the union maintained itself as a potential threat to production.

Labor-Management War, 1879–1887

National revival from the depression of the seventies began in March, 1879, and rose rapidly to a prosperity peak in March of 1882. The trade union movement revived with prosperity, nowhere with more vigor than in Chicago where it was sparked in part by immigrant leaders fresh from the socialist and anarchist movements of Europe.

McCormick wages had been cut five times between 1873 and 1879. In the upswing beginning in late 1879, wage restorations were prompted by shortages of some types of skilled labor and by union bargaining. The period 1879–1882 covers a time of rapid business recovery from the long depression of the 1870's. At the McCormick firm employment approximately doubled from 1879 to 1882 (Profile 5) and profits rose from $722,326 to $1,761,226 (Table 6). These factors alone would seem to be enough to account for the substantial plant average wage increases from 16.2 cents per hour in 1879 to 22.4 cents per hour in 1882. However, the timing of the wage increases to meet union strike deadlines and the bitter company feelings against the Molders Union leads to the conclusion that it was the union and not the labor shortage which was troubling the company.

The union pressure in the early 1880's was exerted as follows. Each spring the city-wide Molders' Union, Local 223, delivered to its 23 Chicago employers a wage increase demand to be met by a certain date on pain of a strike. For example, in 1881 the strike deadline was April 19.

The McCormick firm met this deadline with a wage increase for molders
on April 16. Three of the 23 firms failed to raise wages and were struck.
Employed molders, such as those at McCormick's, were assessed to support the strikes. In 1882 the McCormick firm avoided the usual wage

Profile 5. Labor-Management War: 1879–1887

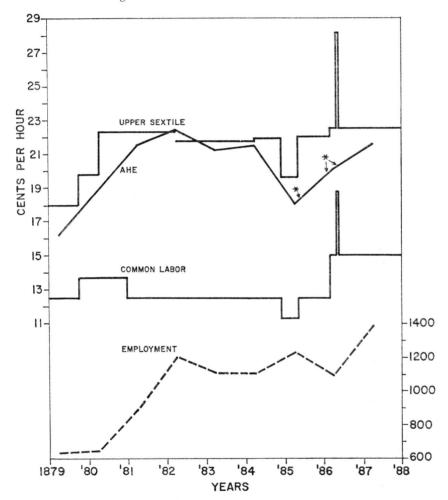

Includes average hourly day rates for skilled labor (discontinuities indicate a change in
the skill mix and not in rates of pay), AHE for the entire plant, the rate for common
labor, and plant-wide employment, 1879–1887, McCormick Works. Asterisks and arrows
indicate strikes.

Source: McCormick Works payroll books, in the McCormick Collection.

TABLE 6

Net Profits, McCormick Harvesting Machine Company,
1879–1898

1879	$ 722,326
1880	1,192,733
1881	1,254,961
1882	1,761,226
1883	1,486,632
1884	1,776,506
1885	841,007
1886	679,924
1887	1,007,767
1888	1,473,986
1889	1,803,319
1890	1,543,037
1891	1,867,058
1892	2,550,322
1893	2,056,481
1894	1,502,581
1895	2,419,978
1896	2,271,184
1897	2,620,930
1898	4,799,811

Source: 1871, letter, C. A. Spring to C.H.McC. I, Sept. 1, 1871, CHMcC I Papers; 1874, letter, Frank H. Mathews to idem, Sept. 22, 1874, ibid.; 1875, letter, Frank H. Mathews to idem, Oct. 4, 1875, ibid.; 1877 and 1878, William T. Hutchinson, *Cyrus Hall McCormick*, 2 vols. (New York: D. Appleton-Century Co., 1935), II: 607, n. 117; 1879, ibid., p. 690, n. 10; 1880–1902, Memoranda, CHMcC II Papers; 1903–1911, U.S. Dept. of Commerce and Labor, Bureau of Corporations, *The International Harvester Co.* (Washington, D.C.: GPO, 1913); 1912–1960, Annual Reports, I.H.Co.

increase by the skilful negotiations of the foundry superintendent, who attended the union meeting and convinced the molders to recede from what Cyrus H. McCormick II called their "suicidal course." [11] It is interesting to note (Profile 5) that in these same years common labor, which lacked a union spokesman, not only was bypassed when the molders received wage increases, but in January, 1881, suffered a pay cut from 13.75 cents per hour to 12.5 cents.

Despite record profits, the McCormick firm cut wages in the recession of 1884–1885 15 per cent for piece workers, 10 per cent for day workers. These cuts dropped the common labor rate to 11.25 cents per hour as compared with the bottom reached in the depression of the seventies of 12.5 cents. After futile attempts at negotiation during February and March, 1885, the molders to a man went out on strike in mid-March,

1885. When the company successfully imported replacements the entire plant joined the strike on April 1.

While McCormick workers were on strike, McCormick's chief competitor, the Deering Harvesting Machine Company, broke the employer front by restoring wages, thus forestalling strikes in its own plant. Workers at the Malleable Iron Company were on strike for only an hour before their wage cut was rescinded.[12] Unable to open its plant, deserted by its fellow employers, the world's largest producer of agricultural machinery capitulated to the unions. Wages were restored.

The across-the-board wage cut of December, 1884, and its restoration in April, 1885, represented an unusual type of wage movement for the McCormick Company. In this era, plant-wide wage movements were not customary. The only precedent for such a move was the across-the-board raise of May, 1867, when the union accepted a 10 per cent increase in lieu of the eight-hour day. Generally, however, in the pre-union, pre-Civil War days, the company had made selective pay changes. Never more than one-third of the workers' wages were changed at any one payroll period. In the depression of the seventies the company, with one exception, alternated its pay cuts between skilled and unskilled, separated by at least several months.

This union victory in 1885 was but a prelude to a more intensified struggle which ended in 1886 with the expulsion of the molders and also the new industrial unions organized in the entire plant during 1885 and 1886. The wage movements during the strikes of February–May, 1886, were phenomenal. On May 1, 1886, half of the new and painfully recruited work force walked out to join the eight-hour-day strikes. The McCormick Company granted a whopping 25 per cent wage increase by instituting the eight-hour day with ten hours' pay. This was in addition to the substantial increases granted at the beginning of the strike in March, 1886, and at the conclusion of the strikes of 1885. Thus common labor rates advanced 66.7 per cent from April, 1885, to May 2, 1886. The eight-hour day increase was rescinded after a few months when police repression following the Haymarket riot destroyed the eight-hour movement.

Post-Union Wage Decline, 1887–1897

This period shows the most unique wage movements of any period since the formation of the company. Average wages, led by sharply declining piece rates, fell almost steadily from 21.7 cents in

1887 to a low of 17.2 in 1895. The wages of skilled craftsmen like the patternmakers rose gradually from 24 cents in 1887 to 25.8 cents at the peak of 1893 prosperity and then fell sharply in the depression to 22.3 cents. Meanwhile, common labor rates, after gyrating wildly from 1858 to 1886, suddenly show an amazing stability through not only the prosperity of 1893 but, what is more amazing, through the first three

Profile 6. Post-Union Wage Decline: 1887–1897

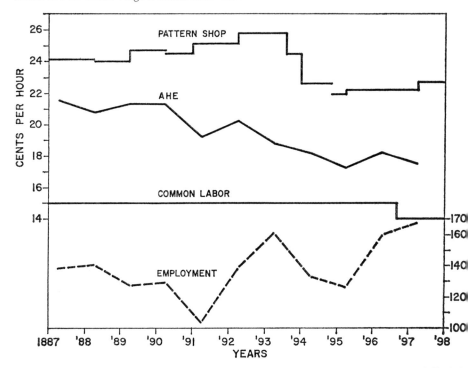

In this and all subsequent profiles the "skilled worker" concept of the "upper sextile" of da rates used in the earlier profiles has been replaced by the "mean hourly rate of pattern sho craftsmen." This change has been necessitated both by the difficulty of obtaining the "skille worker" data when the plant became large and by the unavailability of pattern shop rates prio to 1888. Spot checks from 1888 to 1960 indicate that pattern shop rates moved up and dow at the same time as those of other skilled workers. Chart D-1, "Occupational Differentials the McCormick Works, 1858–1959," shows the similarity of both of these concepts for the yea 1888 to 1896. Discontinuities in the pattern shop rates indicate a change in the mix of high- an low-paid patternmakers, not a change in rates of pay to incumbent workmen.

Includes average hourly day rates for pattern shop craftsmen, AHE for the entire plant, the ra for common labor, and plant-wide employment, 1887–1897, McCormick Works.

Source: McCormick Works payroll books, in the McCormick Collection.

years of the depression. Why were the various classes of labor treated so differently?

The really precipitous wage cuts were those for the molders — from 33.4 cents per hour in 1885 to 18.4 cents in 1891. The most important reason for this was the destruction of their union in 1885–1886. The molders were targets for management because they were by 1884 the highest paid group in the plant. The destruction of the union abolished union agreements on piece rates and all union rules. One rule which the company discarded was that each skilled molder was allowed to supervise only one helper; there had also been restrictions on what tasks the helper could carry out. In 1887 the number of molders went down but the wages of a few went up, in one case to 32 dollars per day including helpers. The skilled molder freed from union restrictions was then supervising the work of a number of helpers and paying them from his own pocket. By 1890 and 1891 the McCormick Company had perfected its own mechanical squeezer so that unskilled men could successfully turn out most types of castings. Therefore, the piece rates of the McCormick squeezer operators were cut further and helpers eliminated. The original mechanical squeezers, which had been installed in the fall of 1885 and which had enabled the company to defeat the unions by utilizing common labor, turned out to be defective and un-economic. The labor market of 1886–1897 permitted successive piece rate cuts so that the big differential between molders and plant average which the molders union had built up over the years — equal to 80 per cent in 1873 and 56 per cent in 1884 — was only 9 per cent by 1895. The introduction of the molding machine and the end of the union went hand in hand. Lastly, the changing technology and the freedom from union rules permitted the breakdown of the operation into simple repetitive operations by unskilled labor, aided by mechanical improvements. Without unions the company was free to take advantage of the favorable labor market situation and it cut wages not only of molders but of such other workers as blacksmiths and woodworkers.

In this period (1887–1897) of falling wages, both money and real, at the McCormick Works, it is clear that the cause was not lowered productivity but the reverse. Startling new inventions such as the pneumatic squeezer in the foundry were highly labor saving since they cut required skills as well as increasing output. If the unions had not been destroyed in 1886, they might have been able to capture some of the productivity gains. Without a union, high productivity in this period simply resulted in growing profits and declining wages.

The really difficult wage policy of this period to understand is that amidst these extensive wage cuts common labor, constituting 36.3 per cent of the labor force in 1886, was exempted completely from the cuts of 1886–1896. Common labor received favored treatment in 1886 because of the lessons President McCormick had learned in the strikes of 1885 and 1886. Much of the public's antagonism to the company in the 1885 strike, he believed, came from his across-the-board wage cut of December, 1884, which aroused public sympathy for the low-paid workmen. In the negotiations preceding the strike of 1886 he had raised common labor rates handsomely. When the 1893–1898 recession began, the McCormick Company, to avoid a repetition of the 1885 debacle, cut only the skilled workers and those on piece rates. Eventually, three years after the depression began, the McCormick firm cut common labor 1 cent, to 14 cents.

Competitive Chicago plants paid substantially less to common labor during this period. The Deering Harvester Machine Company, which had escaped the strike violence and the prolonged strikes of 1885–1886, dropped its common labor rate from 15 to 14 cents in 1887, and to 13.5 cents when the recession struck in 1893.[13] A second Chicago competitor, the Plano Harvesting Machine Company, which likewise had escaped the McCormick ordeal of 1885–1886, paid common labor only 12.5 cents per hour during the 1894–1898 depression.[14] It appears that in comparison with competitors the McCormick Company paid above market rates for common labor from 1886 to 1896 in order to insure labor peace, or at least to gain public favor if labor trouble erupted.

Moreover, labor trouble resulting from wage cuts would have antagonized the firm's largest stockholder, Nettie Fowler (Mrs. C. H.) McCormick, widow of the firm's founder and mother of the firm's president. She had written in 1885 a letter critical of the firm's labor policy, expressing concern for the workers as well as for the McCormick family reputation. Each succeeding labor disturbance in Chicago found Mrs. McCormick harassing the company officials. A year and a half later, at the time of the trial of the Haymarket anarchists, Mrs. McCormick wrote an agitated letter to the officials of the company: "If the sentence is not modified I shall expect that bomb throwing and incendiarism, by individuals, as revenge will be practiced. . . . They have bombs. . . ."[15] In July, 1894, on the occasion of the Pullman strike, Mrs. McCormick alerted General Manager E. K. Butler to the dangers of labor disputes.[16] With Mrs. McCormick in such a nervous mood, it would be a foolhardy executive who would risk labor trouble by slashing wages in view of her remonstrances against the wage cuts of 1884. Despite her advanced age, Mrs. McCormick intervened in favor of Harvester strikers as late as 1913, specifically citing to the International Harvester management the company mistakes of the Haymarket episode.

This recognition of such non-economic factors as "family pride" combined with fear of unionism apparently has had some influence on wage determination. This 1893–1896 example of corporate departure from economic motivation by the McCormick company merely predates by some twenty years the more obvious emergence of fear of public disfavor as a causal factor in the new Rockefeller wage and labor policy inaugurated under the direction of Mackenzie King in the years following the notorious Ludlow "massacre" of 1914. Here a strike in one small isolated Rockefeller enterprise was sufficient to modify the labor policies of the principal Rockefeller companies across the continent, even those with no imminent labor troubles.

The Period 1897–1916: The Wage Impacts of the 1903 Strike and the Presidential Campaign of 1912

The crushing of the unions at McCormick's in 1886 had been followed within a year by the start of a prolonged erosion of wages. Even before the onset of the long depression beginning in the fall of 1893, the average plant hourly rate had receded from 21.7 cents in 1887 to 18.8 cents in the spring of 1893. As piece workers continued to take major cuts, wages reached the depression trough of 17.2 cents per hour in 1895. As in the depression of the seventies, the company profits of 1894–1897 were maintained at high levels. By 1897 profits were already 13 per cent above the pre-depression high of 1892. Wages were still near the depression low, down 15 per cent from 1892.

By 1899 reviving prosperity had affected manufacturing generally. Employment was up. Chicago trade unions were on the march. In 1900 city-wide strikes of machinists and patternmakers, though causing some management apprehension, bypassed the McCormick Company.[17] The great Chicago building trades strike of 1900 slowed down construction of the new McCormick twine mill. Another city-wide machinist strike occurred in 1901. National average wage rates (Chart 1) climbed in 1900, 1901, and 1902. National trade union membership and work stoppages by 1902 almost tripled the levels of 1898.

Somehow through all these strikes and booming employment McCormick wages were barely affected. In March, 1899, the common labor rate was belatedly restored from its depression low of 14 cents to 15 cents per hour, the same level which had been won by the unions in February, 1886, thirteen years earlier. Employment at McCormick's in 1899 rose another 22 per cent above the previous year and in 1900, 60 per cent above 1899. Yet, except for a few selective raises for skilled workers, wages showed little response. As late as 1902 with national average hourly rates rising each year and the trade union membership booming, the McCormick wages were stable for the third year in a row.

There is some evidence that the reason for the failure of the McCormick Works wages to respond prior to 1903 was that in 1901 a newly engaged manager of manufacturing, F. A. Flather, thought he needed to make a good record. Flather's assistant, Brooks, complained to Stanley McCormick that he had been given the following orders by Flather: "Now, . . . I want to make a record for the coming year, and want you to do all you can to reduce your piece work prices. I am sure there are many cases which can be reduced without interfering with output. If you can help me to make a good record . . . I will see that it is to your advantage." Brooks, according to Stanley McCormick, objected to the piece rate cuts because he thought it ". . . bad policy; particularly at the present time when the Unions are making special efforts in our shops, to begin cutting prices. . . . [W]e must expect to pay liberal wages if we desire to keep the shops Non-Union and retain the loyalty of the men." [18]

When unionism finally hit the International Harvester Company in April, 1903, in the form of the Deering plant strike, the business boom was already past. Employment at the McCormick Works, in a reversal of the usual seasonal pattern, fell from 6,118 in November of 1902, to 5,199 in April of 1903. At the 1904 seasonal spring peak it was down to 4,304. Though only one plant, the Deering Works, went on strike, the wage impact on all three Chicago Harvester plants was tremendous. (The wage impact at the McCormick plant is shown on Chart 1 and Profile 7.) In an effort to head off unionism, wage increases were passed out — particularly to skilled workers — in the month of January, 1903. The strike occurred anyway and the union contract called for a several-step reduction in hours from 60 to 54 per week with no cut in pay. This meant an 11.1 per cent wage increase on top of wage concessions already granted. The actual 1903–1904 average increase was 26 per cent for patternmakers, 20 per cent for common labor, and 14 per cent for the entire McCormick plant.

One interesting feature of the 1903 strike was the company's subse-

ofile 7. The Wage Impact of the 1903 Strike and the Presidential Campaign of 1912: 1897–1916

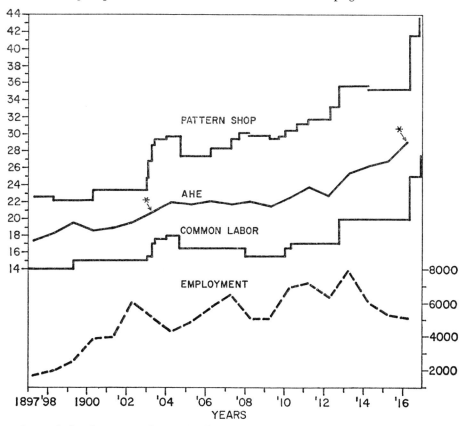

e plant-wide hourly earnings for 1915 and 1916 in this profile are annual averages instead of
e first payroll period in April. These plant-wide annual averages, as well as the employment
ta, came from the records of the International Harvester Co., Chicago. They are, of course,
sed on payroll records, but were calculated by the company and not by the author.
Includes average hourly day rates for pattern shop craftsmen (discontinuities indicate a change
the mix of high- and low-paid patternmakers, not a change in rates of pay to incumbent work-
en), AHE for the entire plant, the rate for common labor, and plant-wide employment, 1897–
16, McCormick Works. Asterisks and arrows indicate a strike.
urce: McCormick Works payroll books, in the McCormick Collection.

quent estimate of how much wages were raised to head off the strike and how much they were raised as a result of the signing of the union contract when the efforts to "buy off" the workers had failed. In 1904 General Manager E. A. S. Clarke put the figures as follows: of a total wage increase of $400,000, $275,000 had been given out in raises to head off the strike and $125,000 in additional raises given out as a result of the union contract. The cost to the company of union-caused wage increases would have been doubled, according to Clarke, if heavy unemployment had not cut payrolls.[19]

When the union contract expired in September, 1904, the company, after weighing all factors, cut back the wage rates about as far as they thought they could without bringing on a new strike. Strangely, the plant average wage dropped only minutely. This was apparently because piece workers put forth greater effort to make up for their rate cut. Skilled and common labor could not escape the substantial cuts. It was eight years before common labor reached and surpassed its 1904 union contract wage. Patternmakers, helped by market shortages, had to wait only three years to be restored to the 1904 level.

The 1897–1915 period was characterized in terms of wage behavior by long periods of wage stability punctuated only by two major wage disturbing events in May, 1903, and October, 1912, and by two minor events in January, 1908, and January, 1910. The stability is illustrated by the failure of wage rates to rise in the tight labor markets of 1906 and 1907. Estimates put unemployment as a per cent of the civilian labor force for 1906 at .8 per cent and for 1907 at 1.8 per cent. This compares with 2.5 per cent for 1953, the tightest year since World War II.[20] The unemployment rate for 1906 was even substantially below the rate during both World Wars. Yet plant-wide wage averages at McCormick's show almost no response to this presumed tight labor market. Common labor rates in 1906–1907 remained stable and were cut in 1908. Piece rate earnings declined a little. Skilled rates rose from 1906 to 1912.

The first wage disturbance of this period was the already described strike of 1903. The second was the political activity of Harvester director, George W. Perkins; its result was a weekly hours cut and hourly pay raise on October 1, 1912. When, in the midst of the presidential campaign of 1912, New York State Democratic Senator Robert Wagner discovered that International Harvester's Auburn, New York, twine mill was violating the hours requirement for women of the New York

State code, the matter became a national political issue because of Perkins' activity on behalf of Theodore Roosevelt. In this case action had to be taken quickly lest Roosevelt's election chances be damaged. The form of the October, 1912, wage increase was to grant the employees Saturday afternoon off at company expense. This was an hours reduction from 58.5 per week to 55. The hourly wage increase was about 2.5 cents per hour, granted to everyone — the first general increase since the union agreement of 1903–1904. But the October, 1912, wage rates merely set a new plateau which was to last three and one half years before the next "earthquake."

A third but minor cause of wage change in the period was the recession of late 1907 and 1908. As of January, 1908, all wage rates were cut 2.49 per cent by dropping the last remnant of the 1903–1904 wage increase. Harvester workers were henceforth to be paid only for hours worked whereas since 1903 they had received a special allowance for hours not worked when the work week was shortened. By April, 1908, the pieceworkers had been able to raise the plant-wide average despite the wage cut of January.

While common labor and piece workers found the 1897–1915 period one of general stability, the small number of skilled workers in the plant found themselves in short supply and saw their wages rise regularly from 1906 to October, 1912. The threat of unionism among the skilled workers was no doubt a factor in these raises. Paul Douglas shows that unionized metal workers in manufacturing with rates well above those at Harvester made substantial gains during the exact years of the McCormick raises to the same trades — 1906–1907 and 1910–1912.[21] After October, 1912, the McCormick pattern shop and other skilled trades went through three and one half years of completely stable wages.

During the 1898–1915 period there seems to have been no systematic manner by which workers could share in the company's prosperity. From 1898 through 1902 the workers were bypassed. The substantial raises due to the 1903 strike came during a period of seriously declining profits. The International Harvester employees failed to share in terms of increased wage rates in the company prosperity of 1908 and the company and national prosperity of 1909.

The year 1909 turned out to be unusually prosperous for the International Harvester Company. Profits had jumped from 10.2 million dollars in 1908 to 16.5 million.[22] It was a long awaited time for "cutting the melon." Stockholders were first in line and were given a stock dividend as well as an increased dividend rate. Executives were given bonuses and a new profit-sharing plan. Cyrus McCormick made a point of not forgetting the workmen. In January, 1910, he put through the Harvester executive board a special resolution on wages as follows: ". . . while we are caring for the stockholder with div. and head men with profit sharing we must not omit the workman — laborers, piece workers, skilled workmen, assistant foremen and foremen — in view of the marked increase in the cost of living which has recently taken place.

"To this end let the payroll be carefully examined again *Now* and any adjustments recommended to put our men in their proper relation to the employees in other places." [23] This unusual wage resolution raised production workers wages about 1.2 cents per hour, well distributed amongst the various classes of workers. It was not, however, a general increase and it bypassed some workers in each department. In total it was substantially less than the union-negotiated general raise of 1903–1904 or the "politically" inspired general raise of October, 1912.

Chart 1 shows McCormick Works wage averages rising in 1913, 1914, and 1915. Actually the last raise (see Profile 7) was in October, 1912. Since plant averages through 1914 were calculated as of April, the apparent 1913 raise really occurred on May 1, and October 1, 1912. The 1914 and 1915 raises were merely due to reduced employment which cut low-paid workmen from the payrolls and also apparently caused pieceworkers to work faster. In fact there were no raises between October, 1912, and the April, 1916, strike. As Profile 7 indicates, wage rates of individual workers hit a three-and-a-half year plateau after October, 1912. In the recession of 1913–1916 the International Harvester Company did not cut wages as it had done in 1904 and 1908, but instead reduced weekly hours to spread the work.

War, Unionism, Inflation, 1916–1920

The World War I period, 1916–1920, makes a sharp break with the relative wage stability of the previous twenty years. The upward spiral beginning in 1916 marked a rise not only in money wages both nationally and at the McCormick Works but in real wages (Chart 1). Whereas the years 1886 through 1915 saw an average annual real hourly rate of increase at the McCormick Works of 0.95 per cent, the years 1915 through 1920 saw an increase of 4.43 per cent. What was the cause of such a real wage rise?

Theoretically, wages rise in inflation because firms, in order to raise production to match increased product demand, expand their employment until a labor shortage becomes acute. From then on, labor turnover rises as workers find themselves in short supply. Firms respond by bidding up wages. Living costs rise concurrently but employer wage responses are not so much due to living cost changes as to worker withdrawal of labor via high turnover or, even more vigorously, to strikes. When we look carefully at the views of the Harvester executives at the time of each wartime wage increase, it is apparent that unionism as well as inflation was a very important cause of the wartime wage increases.

The wartime wage spiral at the McCormick Works did not begin until May, 1916, with a month-long strike — not for cost-of-living raises, but in protest against wage cuts in the forms of a short work week due to slack operations and of piece rate cuts. The strike settlement refused union recognition but granted an hours cut from 55 to 50 per week and substantial hourly pay raises. Common labor received a 25 per cent increase, patternmakers 16 per cent. The average hourly raise was about 11 per cent.

The 1916 strike brought President McCormick so much criticism from Director Perkins that throughout the war he gave wage matters a high priority in terms of executive time, trying especially in the light of Director Perkins' criticism to head off labor trouble by raising wages before serious disagreement erupted.

The Harvester Company granted new general increases of 10 per cent in December, 1916, and anxiously awaited possible new labor troubles in the spring of 1917. Cyrus McCormick's analysis of the labor situation prior to the granting of the 1917 spring raise of 10 per cent was: "The labor situation here is very unsettled. The recent Decision of the Supreme Court upholding the Adamson eight-hour law, and the fact that for the second time the labor interests have held up at the point of the pistol — the threat of strike — [to] the railway managers, insisting that they must have the decision before the Supreme Court rendered its decision — all this will have a very bad effect on the labor situation in the spring. We are carefully considering every point daily with our Manufacturing men." [24] By the fall of 1917 the Harvester Company was still "running scared" of the unions. "The object of the advance" [a 10 per cent raise on October 1, 1917], Cyrus McCormick wrote, "is to bring our present rates up to the union rates." [25] The substantial

Profile 8. War, Unionism, Inflation: 1916–1920

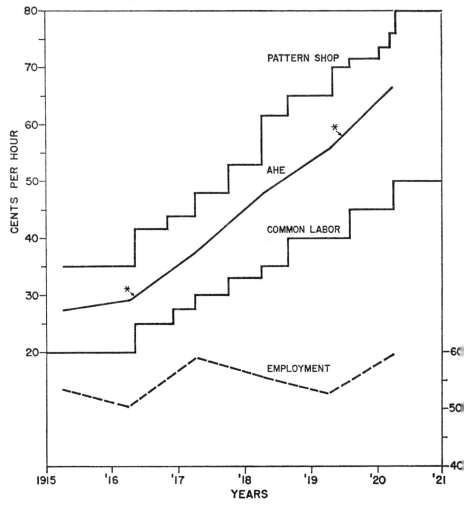

Plant-wide average hourly earnings for this period are annual averages instead of the first pay period in April. Though based on payroll records, they were calculated by the Internatio Harvester Co., Chicago, and not by the author. Employment data are also from Intern tional Harvester Co. sources.

Includes average hourly day rates for pattern shop craftsmen, AHE for the entire plant, rate for common labor, plant-wide employment, 1916–1920, McCormick Works. Asterisks a arrows indicate strikes.

Source: McCormick Works payroll books, in the McCormick Collection.

wage increases of 1917 were given out to meet the twin emergencies of inflation and union organization despite the fact that this was the first year in the company's history to see red ink on the balance sheet.

The spring, 1918, raise was the result of government pressure. Until then the International Harvester Company had refused war contracts because the government required an eight-hour day with time-and-one-half for overtime. Accepting a war contract would force the company to put all its production on the same basis, unduly increasing costs of agricultural implements. As of April, 1918, the Harvester Company reversed its position and went to the eight-hour day. It continued to operate the same 9 hours per weekday and 5 hours on Saturday, but paid overtime at time-and-one-half of the regular rate for the ninth hour. A 5 per cent raise in basic rates was added at the same time.[26]

Another general increase of 10 per cent was granted on September 1, 1918, but in the spring of 1919 the company attempted to economize by skipping common and semi-skilled labor, giving only selective raises to skilled workers. The newly established Works Councils had acquiesced in the company view that wage increases at that time were not necessary. The workers at the McCormick Works, however, had rejected the Works Council plan and joined an AFL federal labor union. They demanded a wage increase and union recognition. In a vain effort to head off the strike the company announced a 10 per cent general wage increase on July 15, the same day the strike began, but made it retroactive to June 30 in all plants with Works Councils. All Chicago implement plants were closed.

Even after the defeat of the federal labor union at the McCormick Works in August and of the AFL Steel Organizing Committee at the Wisconsin Steel Works in October and November, 1919, the labor troubles did not end. On February 18, 1920, President McCormick wrote, "The labor situation seems to be pretty complicated and trouble is feared with the railroad men and we are having sporadic troubles at various works. The other day we authorized an increase of 10% to common labor at some points."[27] In addition to this raise, which was given out to common labor wherever necessary to prevent trouble, all employees received a raise in April. Patternmakers received three increases, one each in January, March, and April.

When the McCormick Works wage chronology from 1916 to 1920 is examined carefully, it is apparent that unionism was a direct factor in the wage increases of what is sometimes referred to as a non-union period. Unionism produced significantly greater wage increases than would have resulted from the inflation alone. These conclusions are based on the timing of the strikes and the wage increases, and upon the statements of McCormick executives. There seems to be no method of quantifying the independent influence of unionism and inflation: the only two other periods of inflation are the Civil War and World

TABLE 7

Membership of Labor Unions and Participation in Work Stoppages, Selected Years

Year	Union membership (1)	Number of workers involved in work stoppages (2)
1903	1,824,000	788,000
1905	1,918,000	302,000
1915	2,560,000	—ᵃ
1916	2,722,000	1,600,000
1917	2,976,000	1,230,000
1918	3,368,000	1,240,000
1919	4,046,000	4,160,000
1920	5,034,000	1,400,000
1929	2,934,000	289,000

ᵃ Not available.

Sources: (1) U.S. Bureau of the Census, *Historical Statistics, Colonial Times to 1957* (Washington, D.C.: GPO, 1960), p. 139.
    (2) Ibid., p. 142.

War II, and comparisons with these periods must be approached cautiously.

In the Civil War, inflation was of about the same magnitude as in World War I and substantially greater than in World War II. Yet wage behavior was substantially different. Nationally, real wages for manufacturing, 1861–1865, fell 30 per cent and rose 30 per cent for 1914–1920.[28] McCormick real wages behaved differently from the national picture in the Civil War, rising 16 per cent 1861–1865.

The union impact at the McCormick Works during World War I was due not only to the influence of unionism among the Works' own employees but to the patterns set by unions nationally. National union growth during this period doubled and the strike incidence rose substantially above the 1916 rate, the first war year for which statistics are available. Strikes in 1916 may well have been several times the 1914 rate.

In the light of the view expressed here as to the significant union impact on World War I wages at International Harvester and nationally, it should be mentioned that one investigator, Albert Rees, has attributed the wage increases in the steel industry in the 1914–1920 period to inflation and not to unionization.[29] In a comparison of steel wage movements in the periods 1914–1920 and 1940–1948, Rees discovered that in the latter unionized period real wage gains were less than in the earlier period. He attributed the wage lag of the 1940–1948 period primarily to long-term union agreements, and the greater wage gains of the earlier period to the impact of inflation on the demand for labor. Rees is probably correct that the unions in at least the 1945–1948 period might have achieved greater wage gains if they had negotiated wage contracts which could have been reopened oftener, say every three months instead of once a year. However, he is probably wrong in implying that the high real wage gains of the 1914–1920 period were due only to inflation and that market demand forces without unions would have brought greater real wage gains from 1940 to 1948. The rapid expansion in union membership from 1915 to 1920 and the phenomenal increase in strike incidence in 1916 and 1919, as indicated in Table 7, show that the powerful union wage impact noted at International Harvester, 1916–1920, was probably just as strong for manufacturing industry nationally.

Illustrative of Rees's underestimate of union wage impact is his crediting to inflation an unusual 1916 situation in which the United States Steel Corporation passed out three substantial wage increases in the course of eleven months.[30] However, George W. Perkins, who was in 1916 a director of both the U.S. Steel and International Harvester Companies, cited to Cyrus H. McCormick II these same 1916 U.S. Steel wage increases as an example of how United States Steel minimized labor troubles in spite of very serious labor disturbances at that time in the Pittsburgh area. Perkins' letter went on to blame Harvester's 1916 strike on its failure to raise wages and then elaborated on U.S. Steel's policy of raising wages to avoid labor troubles.[31]

Clearly 1914–1920 was a period in which inflation and unionism combined their separate wage impacts into a force probably greater than the sum of the separate strengths. The wartime product demand brought rising prices, labor shortages, and high profits. These forces helped bring about militant unionism while softening employer resist-ance. Strikes enhanced the wage impact of labor shortages, and vice versa.

In the period 1916–1920 unionism's wage influence seems to have been felt in three ways. It was felt first through its bargaining strength, the ability to withdraw the labor of the entire plant. During a period of labor shortages and high market demand this was far more effective than in normal times. Secondly, union wage influence was felt through wage concessions by employers who feared being unionized. This mag-nified many times the influence of the rapidly growing unions. Thirdly, union wage influence rose through labor's new-found political influence with the Wilson administration. This last was expressed in many ways, for example, the Clayton Anti-Trust Act, the Adamson Act (whose influence went far beyond the railroads), overtime after eight hours required for war contractors, and the appointment of labor leaders to positions of equality with management on certain government boards.

The Non-Union Twenties: 1920–1932

The major wage interest of the 1920–1932 period centers around the sustained prosperity years 1923–1929. These years are the closest opportunity for comparing non-union wage behavior in a prosperous period with the subsequent unionized period. Not only were there no unions at the McCormick Works or at any International Harvester plants, but even the Works Councils atrophied in the late 1920's and especially after the onset of the depression in 1929. Presumably, from 1923 to 1929 manufacturing industries were more free from unionism than either the immediately prior years, 1916–1920, or the highly union-ized post-1933 period. The period 1923–1929 therefore, is in one sense a laboratory where the operation of supply and demand in the labor market can be observed with relatively little union interference. Of course, even here it has not been possible completely to isolate union influence. Pockets of union influence remained and, more important, the memories of the 1916–1922 trade union upheavals were not easily erased.

A secondary interest in the period is the comparison of wage behavior in two depressions, 1920–1922 and 1929–1932. A third possible interest is the movement of occupational differentials, that is, the relative move-ments of skilled, semi-skilled, and unskilled.

The collapse of wholesale prices occurred in May, 1920. When, seven

months later, the deflation showed no signs of abating, Vice President
Alexander Legge sent a letter to President Harold McCormick to the
effect that a wage cut was now imperative. At a meeting of the works
managers, superintendents protested. They had just completed begin-

Profile 9. The Non-Union Twenties: 1920–1932

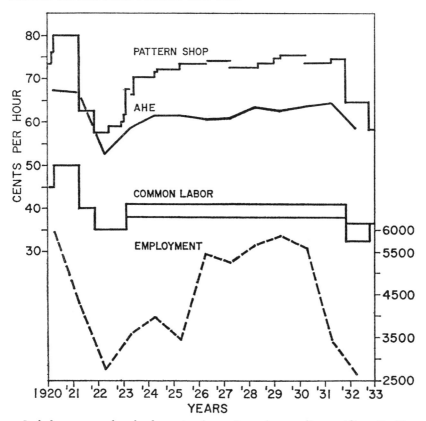

Includes average hourly day rates for pattern shop craftsmen (discontinuities
indicate changes in the mix of high- and low-paid patternmakers, not a change in
rates of pay to incumbent workmen), AHE for the entire plant, the rate for common
labor, and plant-wide employment, 1920–1932.

The average hourly earnings for the entire plant are annual averages for 1920–
1924, and from 1925 are averages for the entire month of April. (See note 2, Chapter 2, for the difference in these two concepts.) These plant-wide average hourly
earnings data and employment data, both annual and for the month of April, were
calculated by the International Harvester Co. and not by the author.

In 1923 two rates were established for common labor, 38 cents and 41 cents; heretofore there had been only one.

Source: McCormick Works payroll books, in the McCormick Collection.

ning-of-the-season piece rate cuts and had promised the workers that there would be no more cuts prior to October 1, 1921. Vice President Cyrus McCormick III, however, stated that the seasonal promises were not intended to cover cyclical changes. Industrial Relations Director A. H. Young called attention to the continuing sharp decline in the cost of living and thought that by March 1, 1921, there would be such an increase in unemployment that the men would satisfactorily accept the wage cut.[32]

In the agricultural implement plants two general cuts actually took place, one of 20 per cent in April, 1921, and a second of 12.5 per cent in November, 1921. The wartime adoption of overtime after eight hours was abandoned. Employment at the McCormick Works by April, 1922, was only 45 per cent of the 1920 peak. Unionism, which had been responsible for two big though unsuccessful strikes in 1919, subsided with the severe unemployment. No outside unions were recognized. Throughout this period the Harvester Company maintained at each plant a local company dominated union, called a "Works Council."

Beginning with the business upswing in mid-1922 and lasting till 1929, there occurred undisturbed by any threat of unionism a continuous competition between labor market forces seeking to raise wages and a variety of company-instituted monopsonistic practices designed to avoid or minimize wage increases. During 1922 and the first half of 1923 the labor market forces seemed stronger. From then through 1929 the monopsonistic forces seeking wage stabilization won out.

In May of 1922 the Harvester Chicago superintendents reported that there was agitation among the skilled trades for a wage increase and that many capable men had left. Although there was no current shortage of workers due to the low rate of operations, the superintendents claimed that if called upon they could not hire skilled workers at the then current rates. A three-man salary committee of assistant works managers, following a study, recommended on May 16, 1922, a 15 per cent increase for skilled trades only. In support of its position the committee prepared a wage survey comparing Harvester rates with those of neighboring plants. Typical was the wood patternmaker comparison: Harvester maximum 74 cents per hour; Crane Company 90 to 95 cents; Western Electric minimum of 80 cents; union rates $1.25. Most plants were on an eight-hour day while Harvester was on nine hours. The most serious labor shortage was for molders. The Harvester plant having the most difficult situation was the southside West Pullman Works which had to compete with the government railroad scale at the Illinois Central Shops and at the Pullman Car Company.[33] This variation in labor shortages in the company's different Chicago plants indicates that to some extent labor markets were neighborhood matters, not even city-wide.

On May 27, 1922, Vice President Legge met with the works managers and flatly turned down the recommended 15 per cent increase for skilled labor on grounds that the product market would not support an increase in prices. The discussion then turned to what lesser adjustments could be made. The result was approval of selective raises for selected workers in skilled occupations to be put into effect with great caution lest the company be faced with a demand for a general increase. In the McCormick Works pattern shop this adjustment raised the average wage only 2 per cent per hour.[34]

By September, 1922, labor shortages were showing in other categories, especially women at the twine mills. Here production was down 15 per cent due to idle spindles and men, who were paid at higher rates, were being used to fill the vacancies. To meet this shortage the works managers recommended that the company rescind its 16-year-old age requirement to permit the hiring of girls 14 years of age. The Industrial Relations Department dissented from the lower age recommendation, favoring instead starting work a half hour later. Both the later starting time and the hiring of 14-year-old girls were adopted. More Negroes were hired because white labor was not available. The above expedients were all introduced because the works managers did not believe that ". . . the solution [to the shortage] is bidding up prices for labor at this time against other manufacturers. . . . [T]he approaching cold weather will increase the supply of factory labor . . ."[35]

But cold weather brought even more acute labor shortages. The super-intendents reported that in the skilled departments some new men were hired at maximum rates, causing resentment among old employees. Good men were leaving. A late 1922 city-wide wage survey by the Chicago Metal Trades Association showed Harvester wages still behind its neighbors. Wood patternmakers in Chicago were then earning 86.6 cents per hour, while the Harvester maximum was 77 cents. Harvester common labor was below Chicago averages. The firm was not attracting good men. Turnover at the Deering twine mill was up to 13 per cent for the month of December, 1922. McCormick twine mill Negro em-ployment had risen from 15 per cent in October to 20 per cent in December, 1922, and still all spindles were not running. In January, 1923, Industrial Relations Director A.H. Young recommended an immediate general increase to get better selection in recruiting and to anticipate the tightening labor market. On January 12, 1923, the works managers, led by Vice President Cyrus H. McCormick III, agreed to recommend to the executive committee a 10 per cent general raise with an extra 5 per cent to skilled workers. The raise took effect February 12. It was decided to put the raise through the Works Councils in order to strengthen them as much as possible.[36]

The general increase did not immediately solve the labor shortage. Other firms were raising wages. In Detroit Henry Ford was reported ready to begin a 10 dollar day for eight hours. By March, 1923, the monthly turnover at the several Chicago Harvester Works had risen to 14.7 per cent from February's 11.4 per cent despite the wage increase in that month. In April the Deering Works and the McCormick Works were short 500 and 400 men respectively with no hope of recruiting that number. The Harvester steel plant was going to Kansas City to recruit Mexicans. Certain works such as McCormick and Deering further increased the percentage of Negroes. Other Chicago Harvester works like West Pullman and Wisconsin Steel continued their policy of hiring no Negroes. Harvester foreign representatives were contacted about directing Swedish, German, and British immigrants to the Harvester plants.[37]

During 1923 the interesting phenomenon of "wage drift" at one plant was discovered by the company. The Industrial Relations Department had established a manual of occupational rates for all jobs in the Chicago plants. This called for a light common labor rate range of 38 to 41 cents and a heavy common labor range of 42 to 45 cents. In June, 1923, the Industrial Relations Department discovered that the Deering Works had put a substantially higher proportion of workers at the maximums than had the McCormick Works. The Deering Works had even gone above the maximum with an unauthorized new classification "extra heavy trucking" at 47.5 cents per hour.[38] Superintendents were concealing high piece rates by a variety of bookkeeping procedures.

By July, 1923, the tight common labor situation at Harvester had eased. Despite serious labor shortages in 1926, 1928, and 1929, the February, 1923, general increase turned out to be the last of the decade. There were a few selective increases in skilled departments between February and June, 1923, and then they all but ceased. How did it happen that during the major part of the prosperity — 1924–1929 — wages were so stable?

Nationally, output per man hour in manufacturing, rising at 4.2 per cent per year from 1923 to 1929,[39] was about double the 1889–1957 average and certainly enough to support far higher wage increases. Nor was there anything in International Harvester's profit picture to explain the wage stability of the period. Harvester's profits rose a bit slowly

TABLE 8

Net Profits After Taxes, International Harvester Company

1920	$16,655,353
1921	4,149,919
1922	5,540,768
1923	10,274,377
1924	13,037,395
1925	19,171,240
1926	22,658,892
1927	23,359,215
1928	29,685,350
1929	36,779,998
1930	25,703,192
1931	1,346,538
1932	− 7,582,879

Source: Annual Reports, International Harvester Company.

at first due to lagging farm purchasing power and to Henry Ford's venture into the tractor business, but by 1926 and 1929 were hitting spectacular highs.

With the decline of immigration after 1914 it is surprising that Harvester wages could remain almost steady during the long boom, 1923 to 1929. Despite the favorable economic conditions the annual average real wage increase at the McCormick plant was only 0.9 per cent per year, 1923–1929, far below the 3.6 per cent rate of the post-World War II period, 1947–1960.

In late 1923 a company survey indicated that though turnover continued high it was chiefly among the floating help. Thirty-six per cent of the employees had tenure of five years or more. During 1924 the labor market remained tight but not critical. Harvester turnover for the year 1924 was the lowest in four years: 1924, 80 per cent; 1923, 177 per cent; 1922, 112 per cent; and 1921, 165 per cent. There was even some discussion of possible wage cuts but nothing materialized.[40] A

March, 1924, wage survey showed Harvester average wages in Chicago about equal to a 60-firm Chicago sample. Union rates, however, were well above Harvester's and had been increased over 1923.[41]

In their effort to avoid being forced to raise wages competitively, the employers in the neighborhood of the McCormick and Tractor Works formed a Southwest Side Employers group which co-operated on wage surveys, and attempted to avoid bidding against each other for short supplies of labor. In 1925 the labor shortage eased but toward the end of that year and throughout the first half of 1926 the skilled labor shortage reappeared. By June, 1926, there was a serious shortage of molders, skilled tradesmen, and to a lesser extent, common labor. No wage adjustments were made. A Chicago wage survey of May 1, 1926, showed that for the third year in a row Chicago wages had remained stable. In fact by December, 1926, even the molders were in such good supply that Industrial Relations Director George Kelday suggested that ". . . the time may be ripe to replace inefficient employees. The first group should be the floaters."[42]

March, 1927, saw much unemployment in Chicago and by May, 1927, the Chicago Harvester plants had no difficulty selecting any type of labor. In the spring and summer of 1928 the labor shortage again appeared, with skilled men hardest to find. It grew worse in early 1929. Again Harvester held the wage line and the situation was corrected by the 1929 recession. By September, 1929, "semi skilled and white laborers" became plentiful. By December, 1929, the skilled labor shortage was gone.[43]

In connection with the compilation of the pattern shop wage data for Profile 9, McCormick Works pattern shop turnover was studied for the period 1922–1929. The results throw some light on the company's labor shortage problem. During late 1922 when the company superintendents were complaining of the high quit-rate of skilled labor, the McCormick pattern shop quit-rate was only 14 per cent per year during the second half of 1922, as compared with 26 per cent per year for the first half of 1924, and 36 per cent annually for the second half of 1928. Moreover, the 1922 "quits" were not the high-paid men and the department was hiring new workers at the bottom of the rate range.[44] Nevertheless, turnover information tells little about quality of workers and the complaints of the superintendents, who were in a position to judge the quality of the gained and lost employees, should probably be given more credence than statistics on turnover. Yet in the years when turnover was really high, such as 1924, 1926, and 1928, no one proposed wage increases. In the twenties it was possible to maintain the work force without raising rates after June, 1923. The biggest increase in the size of the department occurred in the latter half of 1926, employment rising from 63 to 73 patternmakers. This was accomplished by hiring a large block of men at near the minimum rate. In some cases these new men were merely promoted from one of the other metal-working departments of the plant. At the same time, skilled men were hired from the outside, but at middle-range rates. The net effect of the big 1926 recruitment was a drop in the average departmental wage of a little over 1 cent.

A rise in pattern shop average wages occurred between 1926 and 1929 — from 72.8 cents to 75.3 cents. This rise was due solely to the fact that the dropouts (whether quits or dismissals) were primarily from the lower end of the rate range. At the same time that the average wage was rising, the size of the department was declining during 1928 and 1929. Averages of other skilled departments crept up moderately from 1923 to 1929 just as did the pattern shop: the tool room went from 67 cents to 74 cents, the electrical department from 64 cents to 71 cents. These increases were not caused by wage increases to existing workers nor by increases in the top of the rate range; they were caused by gradual dropping out of workers below the departmental averages.[45]

At the McCormick Works common labor averages did not move during the 1923–1929 period. By 1929 there was a tendency for a cluster of rates to form near the maximum of the range, but there was an offsetting cluster of workers at the bottom of the range. The proportion of workers paid common labor rates did not decline during the 1920's.

The semi-skilled departments, which at Harvester were piece workers, fared worst. They tended to remain stable or face slight reductions. The slight gain in the overall average shown in Profile 9 is due to the increases in the averages paid to the skilled workers. It appears from the Harvester Company's wage behavior of the 1923–1929 period that a company faced with labor market shortages has a number of alternatives to a wage raise. At all times the company was communicating on wage matters with other employer groups — nationally with the Special Conference Committee (see p. 96), locally with the Chicago Metal Trades employers, and even with employers with plants in the same neighborhoods as Harvester plants. All of these associations promoted a spirit of opposition to competitive bidding for one another's workers. A second important means used by Harvester to avoid wage increases in this period was to hire members of minority groups and younger girls. Especially the employment of Negroes meant tapping a large new source of labor. A third procedure was to give out wage increases only to selected individuals and departments. When there was no union this could be done without a plant-wide wage increase. Since the success of this procedure depended in part on hiding from some employees what was being given to others, to some extent it created an artificial imperfection in the labor market.

The adoption of a carefully worked out job-evaluation system in 1922 was an effort to establish logical but non-market wage relationships amongst occupations. The system was modified upon occasion since market forces were not easily ignored. The upward wage drift to the top of the common labor range in 1923 is an example of the power of market forces. A second departure from the job-evaluated relationship occurred when skilled rates were boosted half again as much as the increase to common labor during the 1922–1923 upswing.

If Harvester's defiance of market pressures through its reluctance to raise wages during the labor shortage of the twenties seems remarkable, its behavior after the 1929 crash was even more unusual. For two years of snowballing unemployment after the October, 1929, crash the company took no action to cut wages. Strange though this seems, it was merely a continuation of a trend which began in the 1893 depression of delaying wage cuts. Precipitous wage cuts in the depressions of 1873 and 1884 had brought on strikes. From the standpoint of employee morale rather than short-run profits, the post-1929 wage cut delay was sensible. At Harvester, where there had been no wage increases since 1923, an early wage cut would have been disastrous to morale. It would have made a mockery of the company's employee-representation plan.

Big industries like International Harvester behaved during the economic collapse after 1929 as if they were carrying the economic system on their shoulders. Harvester President Alexander Legge, as chairman of President Hoover's Federal Farm Board, was deeply involved with the government's efforts to stem deflation and to maintain purchasing power. In delaying wage cuts in the face of mounting unemployment, Harvester was in company with the biggest American corporations.

Big industry's stable wage and price policies of the twenties and early thirties were reminiscent of the big business philosophy of trust maker George W. Perkins. Twenty years earlier, Perkins had fought within United States Steel for a policy of stable prices in both prosperity and recession. The gradual decline of sales prices and profits after 1929 in contrast to the precipitous declines of the 1920–1922 depression certainly favored the stable wage policy. Lastly, 1931 was the centennial of the invention of the reaper. Much publicity had been put out for this event, including a book by Cyrus H. McCormick III. There were ceremonies across the country. Wage cuts at this time would have been disruptive of the spirit of the occasion. Finally, in October, 1931, the first production worker wage cuts of 15 per cent were instituted. By April, 1932, the efforts of private industry to stem the deflation had been abandoned. A second Harvester cut of 10 per cent at this time marked the complete victory of the deflationary forces. The decline in orders and employment had exceeded any previous recession.

Recent Union Wage Impact: 1933–1960

The year 1933 marks a turning point upward in the long-term rate of wage increases at the McCormick Works. The 1933–1960 annual average rate of real increase of wages is 3.3 per cent, including fringe benefits. This compares with 0.63 per cent for 1887–1914 and with 1.6 per cent for 1887–1932.

This period is characterized especially after World War II by regular general wage increases. In non-union periods increases were usually individual matters and in total amounted to much less than the general wage increases. During World War I general increases were for the first time used frequently, but they were irregular as to timing. After 1945 the increases were timed to coincide with the annual, and after 1950, with the quarterly dates as set by the union agreement. It appears to be the regularity of wage increases of this period that accounts for the high real rate of increase. In the non-union periods wages often remained stable for long periods, for example, 1923–1931.

The national wage picture from 1933 to the present is much better known than for earlier years. Increased federal government action and widespread unionism function in the full glare of publicity. The Bureau of Labor Statistics has in this period made more comprehensive wage surveys. The result has brought much more unanimity in wage movements. Chart 1 shows how McCormick and national manufacturing averages have stayed closer together than at any time in the past, with the exception of World War I, which in this respect was a preview of the future.

Profile 10. Recent Union Wage Impact: 1933–1940

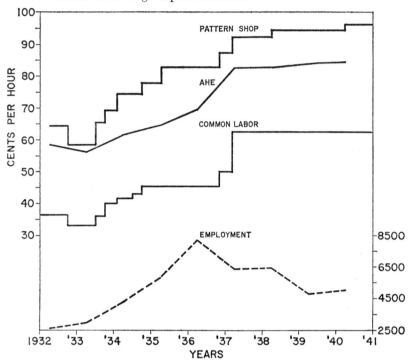

Includes average hourly day rates for pattern shop craftsmen, AHE for the entire plant (computed by International Harvester Co., Chicago), the rate for common labor, and plant-wide employment, 1932–1940 (computed by International Harvester), McCormick Works.

Source: McCormick Works payroll books, in the McCormick Collection.

The first wage upturn in 1933 was the result of the NRA re-employment drive, which cut hours. Subsequent raises in the 1930's were primarily granted to prevent outside unionism from getting a hold. As early as 1933 and 1934 the Harvester "Works Councils," moribund during the late 1920's and early 1930's, took on new life, stimulated by the efforts of outside unions to organize International Harvester Company plants. Unless the "independent" or "company" union at the McCormick Works brought home similar wage increases it would have been quickly tossed aside. The big raise in March of 1937 was clearly to block the threat of the CIO organizing drives which had been so successful in auto, steel, and rubber. The recession of 1937–1940 brought a wage plateau as employment moved steadily downward from the 1936 peak. The active organizing threat of the Farm Equipment Workers Union, CIO, prevented a wage cut despite the business decline in late 1937. Actual bargaining at the McCormick Works with the CIO did not begin until 1941.

The high rates of unemployment in the national labor market make

file 11. Recent Union Wage Impact: 1940–1950

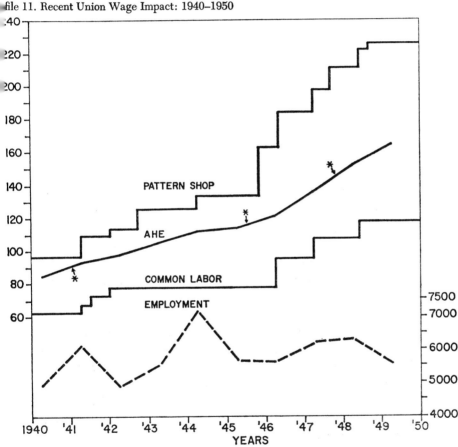

cludes average hourly day rates for pattern shop craftsmen, AHE for the entire plant, the rate
r common labor, and plant-wide employment, 1940–1949, McCormick Works. Asterisks and
rows indicate strikes.

Beginning with 1941, the plant-wide average hourly earnings data are straight-time average
urly earnings. Heretofore, the inclusion of overtime has been of little significance since there
s very little overtime paid, with the exception of 1918–1920. In these profiles we are more
ncerned with basic wages than with temporary variations in overtime.

urce: McCormick Works payroll books, in the McCormick Collection.

it clear that the wage raises of the 1930's were not given because of labor market stringencies.

During World War II the plateau in day rates was set by the National War Labor Board. Common labor was granted nothing after January, 1942. The patternmakers and other skilled trades received two additional NWLB-granted raises in November, 1942, and in April, 1944. There was no plateau in McCormick Works average earnings because the semi-skilled piece workers earnings rose steadily in accord with War Labor Board policy. In the post-war years strikes and inflation pushed wages upward, though for 1947 price increases temporarily cut real earnings.

The post-World War II period was the first time at the McCormick Works since 1886 that unions established regular bargaining relationships. Notable are the regular annual wage increases of this period. The only exception was in the recession of 1949. The regular annual wage increases beginning with the post-World War II period are a contrast to the earlier non-union periods when wages stood still for long periods or declined in recessions. Pattern shop increases had slightly different timing from the increases of the rest of the plant because in some years the Pattern Makers League, AFL, had different contract expiration dates from those of the FEW and UAW, the major plant unions. The patternmakers from time to time during this period got larger increases than those negotiated for the less skilled workers, presumably on the grounds that wage differentials between skilled and unskilled had declined unduly during the thirties and forties.

In the 1950–1960 period the major wage innovation was the quarterly wage adjustment in accordance with the cost of living. This simply followed a pattern set by the United Auto Workers and General Motors in 1948. From time to time special wage adjustments were made to maintain the differential between common labor and skilled workers since the flat amount cost-of-living adjustments had a tendency to narrow differentials.

The frequency of strikes is one indication of the tremendous bargaining pressure which the union exerted on the company during these years. There were strikes during 1941, 1946, and 1948. In the following period, 1950–1960, strikes occurred in 1950, 1952, 1955, and 1958. In addition, in the late 1940's and early 1950's there were hundreds of wildcat work stoppages.

Like the national pattern, the McCormick Works wages of the 1950–

file 12. Recent Union Wage Impact: 1950–1960

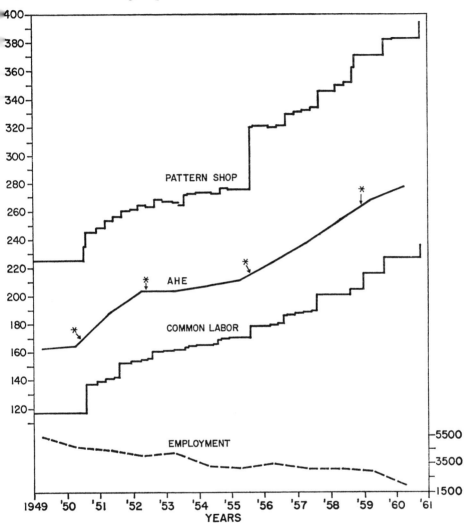

cludes average hourly day rates for pattern shop craftsmen (discontinuities indicate a change
the mix of high- and low-paid employees, not a change in wage rates), AHE for the entire plant
omputed by International Harvester Co., Chicago), the rate for common labor and plant-wide
ployment, 1949–1960 (computed by International Harvester), McCormick Works. Asterisks
d arrows indicate strikes.

urce: McCormick Works payroll books, in the McCormick Collection.

1960 period no longer declined in recessions. In the 1953–1954 recession and in the 1957–1958 recession wages continued their upward march due to long-term union contracts.

Of very considerable significance is the close coincidence of Harvester and auto bargaining patterns. Harvester wage rates and fringe benefits have moved forward between 1947 and 1960 about as rapidly as the vastly more profitable auto industry. Average Harvester net profits after taxes as a per cent of investment, 1947–1955, have been 8.7 per cent as compared with 24.0 per cent for General Motors on the same basis. Under union leadership of the past twenty-five years almost compulsory tandem bargaining relationships with the auto industry have evolved. To disturb these relationships is to invite a prolonged strike.

The outstanding conclusion of Chapter 2 is the important role of unionism in upward wage movement over the last hundred years. Time after time both the McCormick payroll books and the company correspondence testify as to the exact confluence of these occurrences. In 1903 and 1904 the company even calculated exactly the cost of the union contract plus an amount for the wage raises given by the company to avoid unionism. On the exact date of the expiration of the contract, October 1, 1904, the wages were cut back. Profile 5 illustrates the wage gyrations during 1885–1886, which were timed exactly with strikes, collective bargaining negotiations, and the destruction of unions. This timing cannot be explained by cyclical market demand. The very existence of plant-wide wage increases cannot be explained by market demand for labor which could not affect all types of labor in the same way at the same time.

In the subsequent chapters the various causes of wage movement, market demand for labor, productivity, and the product market are considered alongside unionism.

3

Wage Movements for Three Competitive Agricultural Implement Companies, 1882-1902

To check the conclusions of Chapter 2 it would be ideal to have available payroll books of other companies. Fortunately the McCormick Collection contains payroll books for about twenty years of two McCormick competitors producing identical products, one of them located in the Chicago labor market and the other thirty-five miles away. Thus we can examine day-to-day wage behavior of three different firms producing identical products, with two of the three in precisely the same labor market. Moreover, of these three firms, only the McCormick firm was unionized at the beginning of the period and its unions were destroyed in 1886. Thus we can observe wage changes of similar firms under varying conditions of unionization.

Next in size to the McCormick Company was the Deering firm. This company had originated in the mid-1860's in the small town of Plano, Illinois, thirty-five miles southwest of Chicago. In 1880 it moved its plant and key employees to Chicago. It was almost as large as the McCormick Company. The joining of these two giants plus three smaller companies made possible the 1902 merger which formed the International Harvester Company.

When the Deering Company left Plano in 1880, an ex-Deering salesman helped form a new company, the Plano Harvesting Machine Company, to take over the old Deering factory using workmen who had not moved to Chicago with the Deering Company. The new company,

Chart 2. AHE in Deering, Plano, and McCormick Harvesting Companies, 1882–1908

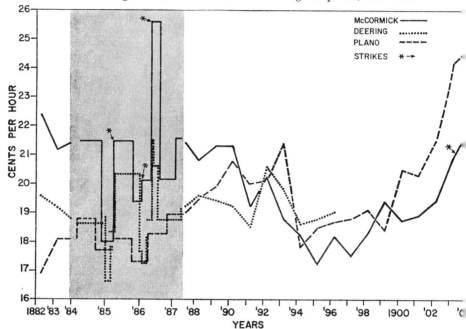

Includes comparative average hourly earnings in three agricultural implement companies, annu
observations (April) for 1882–1883 and 1888–1904, actual wage changes for 1884–1887. Disco
tinuities due to wage changes other than change in day rate.

Sources: McCormick wages, payroll books McCormick Harvesting Machine Co., 1882–1902, a
International Harvester Co., 1902–1904.
    Deering wages, payroll books Deering Harvesting Machine Co., 1882–1896.
    Plano wages, payroll books Plano Harvesting Machine Co., 1882–1902, International Harves
Co., 1902–1904.
    All payroll books in the McCormick Collection.

organized in 1881, was outstandingly successful and having outgrown its
plant by 1893 followed the example of the Deering Company by building a new Chicago plant and transferring its machines and key personnel
from Plano for the start of the 1894 season. Along with Deering and
McCormick, the Plano Company was one of the five original companies
which founded the International Harvester Company.

    Utilizing the payroll records of these three companies Chart 2 gives
comparative wage data for the three competing companies making
identical products. It indicates that from 1882 through 1890 the McCormick Company paid wages substantially above those of its competitors.
(Because of the unusual wage gyrations from 1884 through 1887 the

section of Chart 2 for those years has been enlarged and converted to a profile format in order that we might follow closely the timing of the wage changes.)

To understand this period it is necessary to know the status of unionism in each of the three plants, since the wage movements of two of the three firms, McCormick and Deering, were tied closely together by union activity. Prior to 1887, the McCormick Company had a very strong union of long standing in the foundry. In addition, during 1885 and 1886 the entire plant was unionized by the Knights of Labor and the United Metalworkers Union. All unions at McCormick's were destroyed by the end of 1886 as a result of three bitter strikes — one in 1885, two in 1886 — and of the police repression following the Haymarket riot. At Deering the unions were never so strong. Molders' Union, Local 233, had members in both the Deering and McCormick foundries but was unable to maintain union discipline over its Deering members. On two occasions, 1883 and 1886, Molders' Local 233 expelled from membership some of its Deering members for using more than one helper, "for running bucks" was the union charge.[1] The expelled members continued to "run bucks" at the Deering foundry. Deering Company molders had belonged to a union before the company moved to Chicago. In fact, the Deering foundry foreman in Chicago had been an officer of the Plano, Illinois, molders' local. This local in Plano seems to have disintegrated shortly after the Deering Company moved to Chicago because at the Plano Company from 1881 to 1893 there is no evidence of union activity, though some of the molders had been union members when Deering operated the plant in the seventies.

The wage cuts (Chart 2) of 1884–1885 were the result of the economic recession. The first cut occurred in October, 1884, in the non-union Plano Company. It was selective and applied only to skilled labor. The McCormick Company was next to cut in mid-December with an across the board cut of 15 per cent for all piece workers and 10 per cent for all day workers. Though the McCormick Works had a strong union in the foundry, the cut was made without consultation with the union. The Deering cut was made in January, 1885. The McCormick union was sophisticated enough not to fight back until the peak of the production season. It therefore went on strike on March 20, 1885, demanding the restoration of the wage cut. The very next day the Deering Company restored a part of the cut, which occasioned bitter comments by President Cyrus McCormick about the desertion of his fellow employer.

When the McCormick strike ended in April with a union victory, Deering restored remaining cuts and gave a wage increase besides. The Plano Company, thirty-five miles outside Chicago, did not feel the impact of the union victory, though its average hourly earnings rose slightly due to higher incentive earnings.

New cuts occurred in late 1885 and early 1886. The reduced average wage at McCormick's of November, 1885, was not a cut in rates of existing employees, but the result of replacing the skilled unionized molders with pneumatic squeezers and a large number of unskilled workers. The Deering and Plano cuts were actual wage cuts. The Deering cuts were probably a response to the McCormick Company's replacement of its unionized molders.

In February, 1886, the McCormick unions successfully bargained for selective wage increases for common labor and for helpers, but their failure to secure a union shop and the return of the union molders brought on a new lockout-strike. This prolonged strike was a failure, but a new strike on May 1 for the eight-hour day resulted in a 25 per cent across-the-board wage raise as hours were cut from ten to eight with no cut in pay. The Deering Company gave a raise in March at the peak of the McCormick strike but did not immediately follow the big May 1 increase at McCormick's. The Deering workers thereupon struck for two days and received the eight-hour day but only a 15 per cent hourly raise. Thus on each of the three occasions on which McCormick workers went on strike there were prompt wage increases at Deering. Following the Haymarket bomb repression unions lost their power. At the end of summer, 1886, both McCormick and Deering returned to the ten-hour day, cutting back wages to the pre-eight-hour level.

The eight-hour excitement probably caused wage increases at Plano, but did not bring about the eight-hour day. The McCormick strikes may also have brought increased demand for Plano reapers. Many Chicago Deering workers had relatives and friends still living in Plano during the 1880's. Therefore, when the Deering plant struck and won the eight-hour day in May, 1886, there was excitement in Plano and a brief stoppage in the foundry. There was never a full-blown strike in the Plano Company and never any evidence of union organization.

The very substantial premium paid to McCormick workers over Plano and Deering workers from 1882 through 1886 is clearly a tribute to the bargaining achievements of the McCormick unions. The differential in favor of McCormick workers in this period cannot be attributed to size of city since both Deering and McCormick were in Chicago. By 1886 the small town Plano workers received approximately the same wage averages as the Chicago Deering employees.

Throughout the 1880's the McCormick firm had paid average wages substantially above its competitors, but with the destruction of the unions the McCormick firm was free to cut wages and replace skilled men with machinery and unskilled workers. By 1891 McCormick average wages had fallen below those of its smaller, small town competitor, Plano, and by 1892 below those of its Chicago competitor, the Deering Company. During the nineties the now non-union McCormick Company paid average wages well below both its competitors.

Surprisingly, the Plano Company was able to make a substantial wage cut upon moving to Chicago in 1894. Plano was able to hire common labor in Chicago at 14 cents per hour compared to its 15 cent rate in Plano. As the depression deepened, Plano common labor rates in Chicago dropped to only 12.5 cents per hour. The McCormick Company, though its average wages were lower, continued to pay its common labor 15 cents throughout 1894, 1895, and most of 1896. It cut some of its skilled workers in the fall of 1893 and more in January, 1894. Deering, though in the same Chicago labor market as McCormick, had been paying 14 cents per hour for common labor since 1887. In September, 1893, Deering cut to 13.5 cents. As the depression continued the McCormick Company made further cuts in piece rates, and demonstrated that although it paid the highest rates for common labor it had the lowest average hourly earnings. The McCormick Company cut its common labor rate from 15 cents to 14 cents in late 1896. (See Profile 6, Chapter 2, for an explanation of the differences in common labor rates of the three firms.) It was in its skilled and semi-skilled labor categories that McCormick paid less than its competitors; for example, Deering and Plano patternmakers throughout the nineties received more than those at McCormick's.

There was in the years 1882–1894 in this industry little evidence of a city-town wage differential. In 1882 Chicago wages were above those in Plano, but by 1893 the wages in Plano were definitely above those in competing plants in Chicago.

Wage increases at the end of the depression of the nineties were slow in coming, despite enormous increases in employment. At the Plano Company, now in Chicago, wages began to respond mildly to the increased demand and perhaps to the threat of unionism in 1900 and

1902. McCormick wages were remarkably stable despite sharp upturns in employment. The only big rise in wages in many years came for both firms as a result of the Deering Works strike of 1903 when the three plants were part of the International Harvester Company. The union contract signed with the International Harvester Company as a conclusion to the Deering Works strike applied to the three International Harvester plants in Chicago — Deering, McCormick, and Plano. There were concurrent efforts to unionize the McCormick and Plano Works from 1901 to 1903 and an unsuccessful effort to strike the McCormick plant in 1903. This sharp wage upturn, 1903–1904, came during a severe downturn in employment, indicating that as in 1885 unionism could exert a potent upward influence on wages during deflation as well as inflation.

Chart 2 brings out a number of interesting points. First, although today we speak of a wage differential in favor of the large city, the Plano Company cut its labor cost substantially by moving to Chicago. Perhaps the influx of immigrants prior to World War I resulted in lower labor costs in the big cities. The Plano Company's move to Chicago happened to coincide with the depression of 1893, but it is likely that much of the wage saving would have occurred anyway. Not until 1902 did Plano's Chicago plant wage average reach the rate which the company had paid nine years before in the smaller town. There is another possible cause of the wage decline in Chicago besides a more abundant labor supply: the probability that the new plant incorporated technological improvements which downgraded the skill mix of the work force. New assembly line techniques may have enabled the company to employ a higher proportion of unskilled and semi-skilled labor.

In October, 1902, the Plano Company merged with four other companies to form the International Harvester Company. The big increases in 1903 and 1904 were the same as those given at the McCormick Works. They were due to the International Harvester's efforts to avoid unionism during the union organizing drive and to the union contract which Harvester signed for its three Chicago plants as a result of the strike against it at the Deering Works.

It is interesting to note that though the McCormick, Deering, and Plano companies were all part of International Harvester after October, 1902, Plano wages which had been above McCormick wages remained so at least through 1904. While Plano wages show the same general movements as McCormick wages between 1902 and 1904, the International Harvester Company by 1904 had made no move to equalize wages in its Chicago plants.

Perhaps the most important conclusions from these intercompany comparisons are: (1) Prior to 1887 when the McCormick Company had strong unions its average wages were substantially above those of its two non-union competitors. With the destruction of the McCormick unions in 1886 McCormick wages lost their advantage and in fact became the lowest of the three plants. (2) Wage movements due to strikes at the McCormick Company had very rapid repercussions at the near-by Deering plant but less so at the thirty-five-mile-distant Plano plant.

4

The Wage Impact of Trade Unionism

If unionism is as important in wage movement as the company correspondence and the coincidence of union bargaining pressure and wage
increases imply (Chapters 2 and 3), there should be some way to measure union impact and to compare it with wage behavior in the absence
of unions. The data of Chapter 2 and Table 1 indicated wide variations
in rates of wage growth in different prosperity periods. To what extent
may these varying rates of wage growth in roughly comparable prosperity periods be related to the strength of unions?

To examine this question, Table 9 has been constructed. The essence
of Table 9 is the separation of prosperity periods at the McCormick
Works into those periods in which the plant was unionized and those
in which there was no union. This data is available from the company
and union records for the entire period. The "union" periods of Table 9
are those in which the union was strong enough to be recognized by
the company and to carry out collective bargaining on behalf of
McCormick Works employees. Sometimes the unions were craft unions,
sometimes industrial. In the non-union period there is no evidence of
any union except a "company union" during the period of the 1920's.
For a summary view of the nature of unionism at the McCormick Works,
1858–1960, see Appendix E.

In Columns (1), (2), Table 9, every union period has a higher growth
rate than every non-union period. Furthermore, the average real
growth rate for the 31 years of the four union peacetime prosperity
periods was 3.9 per cent compared to only 0.1 per cent for the 20 years

66

of the three similar non-union prosperity periods. For the money wage rate growth rates at the McCormick Works, union years averages at 3.5 per cent per year likewise far exceed non-union years averages at 0.3 per cent per year. If we examine the number of prosperity years in which real hourly earnings exceeded those of the previous year, McCormick Works employees received increases in 27 of the 31 years, or 87 per cent of the time that the plant was unionized. In the years when there was no union (or only a company union), real wages rose only 11 of 20 years, or only 55 per cent of the time. The five biggest wage increases of the 51 years of prosperity all occurred in unionized periods; four of the five biggest cuts occurred in the non-union periods. The one big cut occurring in the unionized period lasted only three months, when wages were restored as a result of a strike.

Any conclusions based on Table 9 must depend on the significance of the growth rates therein. Are the differences in growth rates amongst the prosperity periods real or can they be due to chance? The best answer to this question has already appeared in Chapter 2 where the exact timing of wage increases with union pressures is far more meaningful than an interpretation of statistical data. The views of McCormick executives as to the important role of unions, while not conclusive, are extremely convincing.

If we apply the F test to the real wage averages of union and non-union periods of prosperity, we get 5.0, double that required at the 1 per cent level of significance. This lends weight to the likelihood that the higher real average wage growth rate in the years when the McCormick Works was unionized were not due to chance.

Since the unionized years were grouped, however, and the selections of years were not random samples, this test does not rule out the possibility that some other factor or factors correlated with unionism were responsible for this different rate of growth. Table 10 gives additional descriptive data on the wage growth rates for real average earnings at the McCormick Works as shown in Table 9.

The standard errors and multiple correlation coefficients of the growth rates of prosperity periods are added in Table 10 primarily for descriptive purposes. The coefficients merely relate each annual movement with the direction of the prosperity period. The standard errors show a wide year-to-year variance in real wages, but this should not be interpreted to mean that no true difference has been established between the average wage growth rates of unionized and non-unionized periods

TABLE 9

Real and Money Wage Growth Rates, Cost-of-Living Changes and Union Status, Selected Periods of Peacetime Prosperity, McCormick Works and U.S. Manufacturing

Period	McCormick Works			U.S. manufacturing			Consumers price index
	Annual percentage rates of growth, AHE production workers, McCormick Works[a]		Union status McCormick Works	Annual percentage rates of growth, AHE production workers U.S. manufacturing[b]		Union status U.S. manufacturing	Annual rates of change
	(1)	(2)	(3)	(4)	(5)	(6)	(7)
	Real AHE	Money AHE		Real AHE	Money AHE		
1865–1873	6.8	2.4	Union	5.0	1.2	Weak but rapidly growing unionism	−3.6
1880–1887	1.4	0.0	Union	3.0	1.6	Rapidly growing unionism	−1.4
1887–1893	−1.2	−2.0	Non-union	1.8	1.0	Slowly growing unionism	−0.8
1900–1903	2.8[c]	4.4	Union	2.5	4.1	Rapidly growing unionism. Av. unionization level 7.2%[d]	1.5
1905–1913	0.4	1.5	Non-union	1.0	2.2	Weak unionism. Av. unionization level 9.5%	1.1

			Non-union	Union	
1923–1929	0.9	0.9	1.1	1.1	0.0
1947–1960	3.6	5.8	3.3	5.3	2.1
					Weak and declining unionism. Av. unionization level 11.4%
					Strong unionism. Av. unionization level 33.3%
Average Union Years[e]	3.9	3.5	3.6	3.3	−0.2
Average Non-Union Years[e]	0.1	0.3	1.3	1.5	0.2
1860–1960	2.0	2.9	2.2	3.1	

[a] See Table 1, for definitions of growth rates.

[b] The designation "union" or "non-union" not applicable here; see (6).

[c] 1900–1903 period for the McCormick Works includes January, 1904, to reflect the wage raises of that month which had been agreed to in the union contract of May, 1903.

[d] Unionization in entire economy as a per cent of non-farm labor force.

[e] Weighted arithmetic average.

Sources: (1), (2), McCormick Works payroll books, in the McCormick Collection; I.H.Co. records, Chicago. Fringe benefits have also been added to (2) on the assumption that they constituted the same per cent of McCormick Works wages as of manufacturing wages.

(4), (5), Clarence D. Long, "The Illusion of Wage Rigidity," *Review of Economics and Statistics*, 42, No. 2, Part 1 (May, 1960): 150–51; *Economic Report of the President*, 1963. Fringe benefits have been added for the years 1939–1958 from computations made by Albert Rees, *New Measures of Wage-Earner Compensation in Manufacturing, 1914–57*, Occasional Paper 75 (Princeton, N.J.: National Bureau of Economic Research, Inc., 1960), pp. 3–4, Table 1, and for 1958–1960 from *Economic Report of the President*, 1962, p. 177, Table 22.

(6), Percentage figures for unionization are from U. S. Bureau of the Census, *Historical Statistics, Colonial Times to 1957* (Washington, D.C.: GPO, 1960), pp. 97–98. Descriptive statements are the judgment of the author.

(7), C.P.I. data from Bureau of Labor Statistics.

TABLE 10

Growth Rates, Variance About Growth Rates and Multiple
Correlation Between Actual and Computed Wage Rates,
McCormick Works, AHE

Period	Real AHE	SE[a]	R²[b]	Union status
1865–1873	6.8	(6.9)	(.92)	Union
1880–1887	1.4	(9.6)	(.21)	Union
1887–1893	−1.2	(6.2)	(.31)	Non-union
1900–1903	2.8[c]	(2.1)	(.72)	Union
1905–1913	0.4	(4.8)	(.11)	Non-union
1923–1929	0.9	(3.4)	(.39)	Non-union
1947–1960	3.6	(2.5)	(.97)	Union
Average Union Years	*3.9*			
Average Non-Union Years	*0.1*			
1860–1960	*2.0*	*(6.6)*	*(.92)*	

[a] The form of the standard error (SE) used here is based on the difference between the computed growth rate for the period and each actual annual change. The formula is as follows:

$$\sqrt{\frac{\sum\left(\dfrac{yo_t}{yo_{t-1}} - 1 - r\right)^2}{N-1}}$$

[b] (R²) shows the relationship between observed data and computed values based on growth rate computed after transferring original data into logarithms.
[c] McCormick growth rate for 1900–1903 goes as far as January, 1904, to reflect the wage raise given in accordance with the union agreement of May, 1903.

Sources: See sources for (4) in Table 1.

or between prosperity and depression average wage growth rates. The basic wage data include the totality of data for peacetime prosperity periods over the one hundred years and big annual variations in relation to long-run average growth rates appear to be characteristic of wage movements. Notice that the standard error of the 1860–1960 period for real AHE at the McCormick Works is 6.6, compared to an average growth rate of only 2.0. The wage data are not samples but are historical time series. Wage movements are frequently highly influenced by wage behavior of the previous year and years. Thus a substantial wage cut sets up expectations and sometimes behavior leading to its restoration.

Turning to the behavior of wages in "U.S. manufacturing," Columns

(4) and (5) of Table 9, one is struck by the similarity of the growth rate trends to those of the McCormick Works. But before interpreting the wage movements, it is necessary to understand Column (6), "Union status for U.S. manufacturing." The statements describing union strength and the direction of union growth are judgments of the author, but for all except the period 1947–1960 are based on descriptions of union activity in *History of Labour in the United States*, II, IV, by John R. Commons and Associates, on BLS figures, 1880–1960; on numbers of strikes and number of workers involved in strikes (see Appendix C); and beginning with 1900 upon union membership as a per cent of the non-farm labor force. Whether unionism was growing or declining was of more actual significance to wage impact than small differences in percentages of the non-farm work force unionized.

When one compares union status at the McCormick Works with that for U.S. manufacturing, it is apparent that for most periods unionism at the McCormick Works was part of a national phenomenon. For five of the seven peacetime prosperity periods listed in Table 9 wage rate movements were of reasonably similar magnitudes for both the McCormick Works and for U.S. manufacturing. The two apparent differences in rate of growth were 1880–1887 and 1887–1893. The lower growth rate at McCormick in the latter of these two periods, − 1.2 per cent as compared with +1.8 per cent nationally, is accounted for by the crushing of the unions at the McCormick Works during 1886 in the events culminating in the Haymarket affair. After Haymarket the McCormick Works for a time changed from a plant in which unionism had been well above average in strength to one of no direct union strength whatsoever.

The second prosperity period showing somewhat differing rates of real wage movement is 1880–1887, when the McCormick Works wages moved up only an average of 1.4 per cent per year compared to 3.0 per cent for U.S. manufacturing. This lower rate of wage growth requires some explanation since it occurred during a period of very strong unionism at the McCormick Works. The lower rate of growth at the McCormick Works is due to two forms of statistical distortion. The cause of the distortion of the figures in Table 9 is apparent from the following raw wage data covering the period 1880–1887 plus one earlier year, 1879.

By looking at the money wage gains from the bottom of the recession, 1879, to the end of the period, 1887, it is clear that the McCormick

Works had a greater simple arithmetic per cent wage increase than the U.S. manufacturing average, 33 per cent to 18 per cent. The highly unionized McCormick Works picked up from the depression much more rapidly than the U.S. average. Our statistics in Table 9 deliberately measure wage gains not from the bottom of the recession but during the more typical portion of the prosperity and hence miss much of the quick response of the strongly unionized McCormick Works.

TABLE 11

Money Wage Changes, 1879–1887, AHE McCormick
Works and U.S. Manufacturing

Year	McCormick Works money wage (cents per hour)	U.S. manufacturing money wage (cents per hour)
1879	.162	.126
1880	.187	.130
1881	.216	.135
1882	.224	.138
1883	.212	.142
1884	.215	.144
1885	.180	.141
1886	.201	.143
1887	.216	.149
Arithmetic Increase, 1887 over 1879	33%	18%

Source: See Appendix A.

During such periods the McCormick wage gains are underestimated in relation to the U.S. average. The statistical technique used in Table 9 (and the other tables) weights its results in such a manner that wage increases bunched in the early years of a period lower the average growth rate.

Taking simple arithmetic money wage gains from 1880 to 1887, the same years as in Table 9, we find 15 per cent for the McCormick Works to 14 per cent for the U.S. average. Again, it is the bunching of gains early in the prosperity period which, with the statistical technique of Table 9, in one sense underestimates the wage growth rates at the McCormick Works.

The low wage figure for the McCormick Works in 1885, Table 11, is also a distortion on the low side. It arose because the McCormick Works wage data are based on one payroll period per year and in this year it was an unrepresentative payroll period, following an employer wage cut and just before a strike which restored the prior wage. The wage rate of 18 cents per hour for 1885 is thus not accurate as an annual average: for three-fourths of the year the wage was approximately 20 cents. When this statistical discrepancy is taken into account, it is clear that every unionized period of peacetime prosperity at the McCormicks had a substantially higher rate of wage growth than the non-union periods.

For the four peacetime prosperity periods since 1900, wage growth rates for both the McCormick Works and U.S. manufacturing were remarkably similar. Thus if unionism is a likely cause of increased rates of money and real wage growth at the McCormick Works, it deserves serious consideration as a possible cause for similar changes in rates of wage growth in the broader area of U.S. manufacturing.

Cost-of-living data are included, (7), Table 9, because they shed some light on the price instability of two of the seven periods. Some of the high real wage growth rates of 1865–1873 period may have been due to declining prices. The rest were presumably influenced by unionism, labor market, and other forces. The only other peacetime period with somewhat unstable prices was the 1947–1960 period. Here price movements ate heavily into wage increases. In this period the achievement at the McCormick Works of a real wage growth rate of 3.6 per cent annually and 3.3 per cent for U.S. manufacturing meant money wage increases of a much greater magnitude.

Table 9 omits data on one interesting period, 1934–1941. This was omitted because the prosperity years — 1936–1937 and 1940–1941 — are too short to establish any meaningful growth rate. The 1934–1941 period has one of the highest periods of real wage growth in the hundred-year history, 5.0 per cent per year at the McCormick Works and 3.9 per cent for U.S. manufacturing despite a very high rate of unemployment. Its union status is not easy to define: during part of the period the workers were represented by a Works Council and for the rest of the time by a non-affiliated local union. Both groups were labeled company-dominated by the National Labor Relations Board, but for the twelve months beginning November, 1936, the workers in the entire plant achieved the second largest peacetime raises ever received, 18 per cent above 1936 (the largest, 25 per cent, was in May, 1886). In 1937 the company appears to have been paying heavily to keep pace with or to better union wage patterns and thus avoid having to deal with an outside union. The company had done the same from January through April, 1903, and during World War I. During these periods unionism was a real threat in the plant, in the firm, and in the country.

Workers at one of the Harvester plants, the Wisconsin Steel Works (located on the south side of Chicago), have remained unaffiliated with outside unionism. In contrast to the frequent strike record at both Harvester agricultural implement plants and non-Harvester steel plants, Wisconsin Steel has had only one short strike since the national steel strike of 1919. Yet every year it gets benefits substantially equal to the pattern negotiated by the United Steel Workers of America. This observation of a period of rapid wage increases at Harvester's steel plant, a period when there was no direct economic pressure such as a strike upon the company, is an illustration of the wage impact of the threat of unionism, and of the very broad wage influence that even a small percentage of union members in the wage force can have if the union movement is growing and constitutes a real threat to other firms. The threat of outside unionism can have a constant effect year after year. This threat is not equal across the country nor across industries. Varying product market conditions, varying personnel policies, and even union-restrictive state legislation singly and in concert may bring about substantial differing wage responses to the threat of unionism.

It is the combined evidence of Table 9 and of the Wage Profiles 1 through 12 which makes the case for unionism as a wage determinant. Perhaps the behavior of the common labor rate from December, 1884, to May, 1903, illustrates (Profiles 5, 6, 7) the nature of the union impact. Due to the depression of 1884 the McCormick Company in December of that year cut the common labor rate 10 per cent, from 12.5 cents to 11.25 cents. The strike settlement of April 7, 1885, restored the cut. In February, 1886, a collective bargaining conference with McCormick management raised common labor rates from 12.5 cents per hour to 15 cents. A lockout and strike followed due to disagreement on other issues. In May, 1886, an eight-hour strike again shut down the plant for the third time in 15 months. The company quickly granted the eight-hour day with ten hours pay, raising common labor to 18.75 cents per hour or a 67 per cent rise over the pre-1885 strike rate of 11.5 cents. Several months later when police repression after the Haymarket bomb had destroyed much of Chicago's union movement, the company went back to the ten-hour day and cut common labor rates to 15 cents, a rate not exceeded until the next strike in 1903. The 1885–1886 wage move-ment was the largest real wage increase in the history of the company.

There have been three types of wage increases given at the McCor-mick Works. The first was the individual raise given out by manage-ment to selected workers or possibly in a few cases as the result of individual negotiation. The second was the departmental raise such as to the foundry or within the foundry to the molders. The third was the general wage increase given to all workers in the plant. The first type, the individual raise, typified the non-union wage pattern; the second and third types were almost exclusively restricted to the union-ized periods.

In the generally non-union period between 1887 and 1933 (excepting the union periods of 1903–1904 and 1916–1919) wage rates tended to remain stable for long periods of time. Thus there was a 15-cent com-mon labor rate from 1886 through 1902, with a cut to 14 cents during 1897 and 1898. Even the rates of the skilled patternmakers were absolutely stable from the general raise of October, 1912, until the strike of May, 1916. All wage rates were again stable from June, 1923, until the cuts of October, 1931.

During the Civil War the Molders' Union struck and earned a raise in wages for the foundry which later spread to the whole plant, but there were no real plant-wide general increases in these years. The first general raise in the company's history occurred in 1867 in settlement of the May Day eight-hour strike, the second in settlement of the strike of April, 1885, the third in settlement of the May Day strike of 1886, the fourth in settlement of the strike of 1903. In settlement of the May, 1916, strike the company gave a general increase and continued with fall and spring general increases for the duration of the war.

Between 1858 and 1933 there were only two peacetime general wage increases not caused by strikes or union bargaining. The first was in October, 1912, when the company for political reasons was forced to cut hours from 58.5 to 55. This was accompanied by a general wage raise. The second peacetime non-union general raise was in February, 1923, when a very tight labor market was met by a general raise; this was the only peacetime general raise ever granted due to labor market shortages. Since 1933 general raises have become the dominant form of raise: following the NRA raise of July, 1933, general raises were given through 1941 to avoid unionism or to match union patterns, and after 1941 as the result of union negotiations. During World War II the War Labor Board controlled wage increases.

The periods of rapid increase in money and real wages were the unionized periods when general increases were the rule. Individually granted raises have never, outside the Civil War, been widespread enough to have had much effect on the plant-wide average wage.

In depressions there has been a growing lag in the period between the onset of the depression and the date of the first wage cut. In 1873 they were simultaneous. By the 1929 depression the lag of the wage cut was two years. By the depression of 1937, and subsequent depressions, there were no wage cuts at all. It is probable that the growing experience with unions which struck against wage cuts in 1873 and 1885 was partially responsible for the increasing lag in wage cuts and largely responsible for the eventual abolition of wage cuts beginning with the 1937–1939 recession. Both the statistical evidence of Table 9, the various Profiles, and voluminous testimony of generations of Harvester executives[1] strongly support the key role of unionism in McCormick Works wage determination.

The desire by non-union firms to avoid unionism results in substantial spillover of union influence to wage patterns broadly. Wages move in patterns which obliterate major differences between union and non-union firms. The unions set the annual patterns which even the non-union firms follow. The regular patterns of annual increases characterize union periods. These union periods without exception have higher rates of real wage increase than the non-union periods.

It is always dangerous to draw conclusions on the cause of the movement of the dependent variable (wages) by looking at only one explanatory variable at a time as in Table 9. However, the restriction of the data of Table 9 to seven periods of prosperity, four union and three non-union, has tended to hold stable two other important explanatory variables — labor market conditions and firm profits.

An examination of the yearly McCormick Works employment data in the profiles of Chapter 2 indicates clearly that the three non-union prosperity periods of Table 9 did not exert less labor market pressure on wages than in the four unionized prosperity periods. Or a glance forward to (3), Appendix B, reveals succinctly this same conclusion for the period since 1900 based on national labor market data. That profits were not more favorable to wage increases during the union periods can be checked for six of the seven periods in Table 27 of Chapter 7. Had data for all independent variables been available for all hundred years, a multiple regression equation might have been constructed. The present method, however, by examining union influence in prosperity does give a form of simultaneous attention to the major variables.

rt 3. The Ratio of McCormick AHE to U.S. Manufacturing AHE, 1860–1960; Sector Value
:puts in Agriculture and Manufacturing, 1869–1957

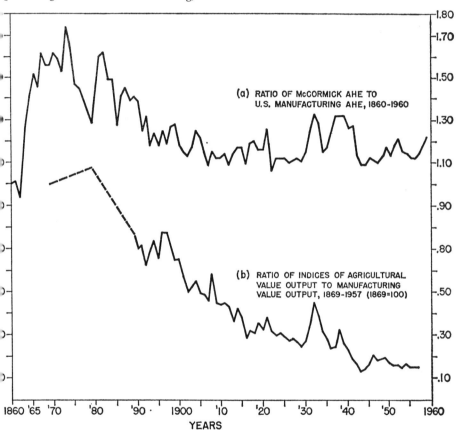

ludes wage ratio and sector output comparison, 1860–1960: (*top line*) ratio of AHE at the
Cormick Works to AHE for U.S. manufacturing; (*bottom line*) ratio of agricultural value
:put to U.S. manufacturing value output.

rces: *top line*, see Appendix A.
ottom line, John W. Kendrick, *Productivity Trends in the United States* (Princeton, N.J.:
nceton University Press, 1961), Table B-1, Column 1, pp. 362–64, and Table D-11, Column 1,
. 465–66.

Depressions are too variable in magnitude and duration for this same treatment and are treated more simply in Chapter 5.

In Chart 3 and in Chapters 5–7 an effort is made to examine additional data which might indicate other possible causes of wage movement and thereby to modify or verify the important role of unionism in wage rate growth which the data of Chapters 2 and 3 have thus far indicated.

Looking first only at the top line of Chart 3, McCormick wages relative to U.S. manufacturing wages, we see that in the early years, 1862 to 1890, McCormick wage levels held a substantial margin over U.S. manufacturing wage levels. This was the period when the McCormick Works was much more highly unionized than manufacturing as a whole. The decline in the ratio from 1882 to 1887 is perhaps due to the catch up of unionism in U.S. manufacturing in relation to the already unionized McCormick Works. The continued decline of this ratio from 1887 to roughly 1910 may be due to the destruction of unionism in the McCormick Works in 1886. The temporary reunionization of the McCormick Works from 1902 to 1904 is reflected in the rising ratio of those years. After 1910 it remained stable except for a relative McCormick wage rise in World War I and a delayed McCormick wage cut during 1920 and 1921. In the thirties there was a double spurt in the wage ratio, first during the downturn, 1929–1933, caused as in 1920–1921 by the slowness of International Harvester to cut wages, and during 1936–1941 when the hot breath of the CIO sparked big wage increases, especially in 1937. A small spurt occurred from 1955 to 1960 because International Harvester was forced by the union to follow the automobile industry wage pattern. But for the most part McCormick Works wages have maintained an almost constant relationship to manufacturing wages since about 1900. It is also true that in this period the strength or weakness of unionism at the McCormick Works coincided with the trends in U.S. manufacturing.

Though giving a continuous picture of McCormick and U.S. manufacturing wage relationships, the wage ratio line adds little to the growth rate information of Table 9, except perhaps the wage relationships in the depressions. These are probably significant only as illustration of the existence of a big industry pattern of delaying wage cuts in depressions.

The bottom line, Chart 3, is a ratio of agricultural value output to manufacturing value output. It is included merely to learn if its movement might help explain the movement of the McCormick and U.S.

manufacturing wage ratios in the top line. Although the data are only at ten-year intervals from 1869 to 1889, their movement does coincide in the early years with the wage ratio line above. It is thus possible that the higher wage growth of the McCormick Works in the pre-1887 period relative to wages in U.S. manufacturing might be due not to greater unionism but merely to the relatively great market demand for agricultural machinery which may have created above average demands for labor at the McCormick Works. However, the divergent directions of the two ratios, wage ratio and value output ratio, from 1900 to 1957 indicates that there is no consistent relationship between them. Despite the agricultural sector's almost steady decline since 1900, McCormick Works wages kept their lead over manufacturing wages. This implies that other factors are better explanations of wage movements than relative sector value output.

The elimination of agricultural and manufacturing value output ratios as an explanation of wage movements re-enforces the important wage influencing role of unionism as indicated in the wage growth rate analysis of Table 9, though it is still possible that the rate of mechanization of agriculture may have been fast enough to cause a more than average increase in demand for labor in agricultural machinery.

Hours of Work

Modern union leaders calculate reductions of hours worked in terms of the per-hour value involved, and are willing to accept small annual pay increases in lieu of slightly reduced hours of work. This is relatively new, however. In the McCormick Works historically, decreases in hours worked ordinarily have been accompanied by wage increases adequate to maintain weekly pay unchanged.

In 1848 the work week at the newly opened McCormick Works was 60 hours. A strike on May Day, 1867, for the eight-hour day failed: the union took a 10 per cent wage raise and no decrease in hours. A similar strike in 1886 reduced hours to 48 with no decrease in pay, but the gain was short lived. An attempt by the Harvester Company in 1903 to forestall a strike for the nine-hour day failed, and from January to September, 1904, hours held at 54 per week with wages at the former 60-hour level. In September hours went back up to 58.5 per week; hourly wages were cut proportionately but weekly wages were not.[2]

In October, 1912, as a result of unfavorable publicity in the presi-

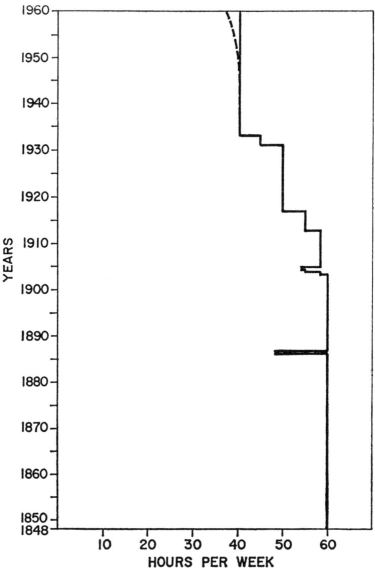

Chart 4. Weekly Hours at the McCormick Works, 1848–1960

Dotted line beginning in 1933 represents estimated reduction in working time for vacation, holidays, wash-up time, coffee breaks.

Source: Payroll records, McC.H.M.Co. and I.H.Co., McCormick Collection.

dential campaign of 1912 due to long hours of work for women in twine mills, the International Harvester Company cut the work week from 58.5 hours to 55. A near proportionate general wage increase was given.

The April, 1916, strike was settled with a weekly hours cut, 55 to 50, and a proportionate across-the-board raise. The work schedule was then nine hours on weekdays, five on Saturday. Up to this point wage increases incident to hours reductions or attempted hours reductions (1867) were almost the only plant-wide raises ever given. The exception was the across-the-board wage restoration after the strike of 1885.

During World War I participation in government contracts required a basic eight-hour day. In April, 1918, therefore, Harvester began payment of overtime after eight hours a day. It did not otherwise alter the work week of 50 hours. The accompanying raise in basic hourly rates was only 5 per cent. This was not a real cut in the work week since there was no increase in leisure and the 50-hour week continued into peace time. When the eight-hour day as a basis for overtime was dropped in 1921, no change in the 50-hour work week occurred.

During the post-1929 depression the first work week cut, 50 to 45 hours, was made without a commensurate pay raise. It was a management decision made for the purpose of sharing unemployment. Not even the Works Council was consulted on this change.

The last change was made in 1933, when the 40-hour week was established along with an 11.1 per cent raise through the setting up of NRA codes. This raise did not quite compensate in weekly pay for the cut in hours. Likewise in this hours change, the national government's policy rather than overt pressure by Harvester workers was the reason for this change.

The regular work week in Chart 4 is not a total picture of actual hours worked. Throughout Harvester history prior to the Fair Labor Standards Act of 1938 the actual hours worked by piece workers varied somewhat from the stated work week. In the early days molders worked until the furnace had been emptied of molten metal. This seldom coincided exactly with the ten-hour day. In 1926 one company executive upon a 4 A.M. morning visit to the Deering Works foundry discovered it in operation. Upon inquiry he learned that some molders began work as early as 1 A.M. in order to increase piece work earnings. This early starting hour was, of course, common knowledge to the foundry superintendent. At a Works Managers meeting it was seriously proposed to extend the informal early starting time to the McCormick foundry in order to cut down turnover by permitting larger weekly earnings.[3] The proposal was eventually vetoed as not likely to have the desired effect.

The dotted line at the top of Chart 4 indicates the gradual increase in leisure via paid vacations and holidays, while the work week remains nominally at 40 hours per week. If on Chart 4 we replace time with annual income, we get symbolically the typical backward sloping supply curve for labor. It is significant to notice how abruptly leisure lost its utility after the 40-hour week was reached. The slow backward bend below the 40-hour week indicates the way the increased vacations and holidays are moving toward fewer annual hours of work.

Historically at the McCormick Works unions were the chief force behind the reduction in the work day and work week. The depression of the early 1930's and the NRA were additional forces for cutting the work week. The recent reductions in hours of work through vacations, holidays, and rest periods at the McCormick Works are overwhelmingly due to union pressures and can be clearly traced in the labor agreements negotiated since 1941.

5

The Wage Impact of Market
Demand for Labor

The data in Table 1 indicate substantially lower rates of wage gain in periods of extreme labor surplus (major depressions) than in periods of prosperity or wartime. Thus in money terms, for U.S. manufacturing 51 years of peacetime prosperity show an average growth rate of 2.6 per cent to —4.0 for 17 years of major depressions. For the McCormick Works the averages were 2.2 per cent in prosperity and —4.8 in depressions. This is what one would expect. But what is surprising is the major conclusion of this chapter that, with the exception of major depressions, market demand in peacetime was a chronically weak force on wage movements over the hundred-year period.

The correlation, r, for annual percentage changes in money average hourly earnings with percentage employment changes at the McCormick Works, 1860–1960, is .18, significant at the 5 per cent level. This may be interpreted as a weak response in the expected direction. Lagging wages a year behind employment changes, 1860–1959, dropped the correlation to .17, still significant at the 5 per cent level.

There is no theoretical reason why firm wage changes should correlate closely with firm employment changes. Instead, the firm's wages should be related to the community labor market situation. Yet both the firm employment changes and the community labor markets are closely related to the national trends. All national depressions hit the International Harvester Company. William Bowen has correlated national unemployment rates with U.S. manufacturing wage changes, 1900 through 1958. He found the correlation, r, too low, —.18, to be significant.[1] If national wage and labor market conditions are so loosely related, it is not surprising to find the weak correlations between the McCormick Works wage and employment trends.

An inspection of McCormick Works annual employment and wage

TABLE 12

Wage Increases in the Same Years as Employment Declines: Change Over Previous Year in McCormick Works Employment and Wages, Nature of Union Activity, and National Unemployment, Selected Years

Year	Annual per cent employment change in McCormick Works (1)	Annual per cent change in AHE (money) McCormick Works (2)	Nature of union activity (3)	National un-employment as a percent of non-farm employees (4)
1867	−19.2	14.0	Strike	—[b]
1886	−11.0	11.7	Strike	—[b]
1903	−15.0	7.7	Strike	4.4
1904	−17.2	5.3	Union contract	7.9
1937	−22.9	18.7	Union pattern	20.0
1949	− 7.5[a]	7.9	Union contract	7.3
1954	−17.0[a]	1.0	Union contract	6.3
1958	− 8.2[a]	8.0	Union contract	8.4

[a] Based on company-wide employment changes, since at the aging McCormick Works employment declined more than that of the firm.
[b] Data not available.
Sources: (1), (2), and (4) in Appendix B.

changes, 1860–1960, in Appendix B gives several clues as to factors which interfere with the expected correlation between employment and wage changes. The first of these is trade unionism.

There were eight years when sharp employment declines were accompanied by wage increases. These are listed in Table 12, along with the national labor market data and some information on unionism.

In the years listed in Table 12 union pressure apparently overcame market wage pressures arising from the firm's employment trends. Nor can the wage increases of (2) of Table 12 be accounted for by the national labor market condition as indicated in (4), since for all the years except 1903 they indicate depression levels of unemployment.

The wage chronologies, Chapter 2, indicate that all the raises of Table

12, except 1937, were the result of direct union action and the 1937 raise followed union patterns in steel and auto industries. The 1949 raise was not an actual raise during 1949 but was the result of a union negotiated raise in the late summer of 1948. The union contract prevented a cut when the 1949 business downturn occurred.

The data of Table 12 imply that the correlation between employment changes and AHE changes should thus be less during unionized periods. This is in fact the case. The correlation, r, for 50 peacetime unionized years was .04 (not significant) and for 35 peacetime non-union years .40 (significant at the 5 per cent level). This further implies that market demand was a more potent force in influencing wages when it was not influenced by unionism.

TABLE 13

Wartime Wage Employment Relationships: Wages and Employment Changes at the McCormick Works and National Wartime Unemployment Rates, Three Wars

Year	Annual per cent change in AHE at the McCormick Works	Annual per cent change in employment at the McCormick Works	Unemployment as a per cent of non-farm employees
CIVIL WAR			
1861	3.2	−13.1	—[a]
1862	1.0	1.8	—[a]
1863	36.4	−10.8	—[a]
1864	25.9	99.5	—[a]
1865	20.0	−26.7	—[a]
WORLD WAR I			
1915	2.3	−11.8	14.3
1916	8.6	−5.1	7.1
1917	28.9	16.3	7.0
1918	27.2	−5.5	2.1
1919	16.4	−5.2	3.4
WORLD WAR II			
1941	10.8	23.5	13.3
1942	4.8	−20.4	6.3
1943	8.0	12.4	2.5
1944	8.4	30.0	1.6
1945	3.2	−21.0	2.5

[a] Data not available.

Sources: See Appendix B.

Besides unionism, wartime distorted the expected wage and firm employment relationship. In all wars the labor shortages meant employment declines coinciding with wage increases. Thus in three of the Civil War years, see Table 13, wages rose while firm employment contracted. In World War I, employment dropped in four of the five years. In three of them, 1917, 1918, 1919, the wage increases were extremely high. There was less tendency for this to occur in World War II because of more rigid wage and manpower controls. Yet eliminating the war years, 1861–1865, 1915–1919, and 1941–1945, raised the correlation, r, from .18 to only .22. As might be expected, national labor market data, (3), Table 13, is a better explanation of the firm's wage behavior in wartime than firm employment movements.

A third reason for the lack of close correlation between wage and employment changes is the fact that the Harvester firm was occasionally able to make enormous increases in employment with no increase and sometimes a cut in average hourly earnings. Table 14 lists the years in which this occurred, the firm's wage and employment movements, and the national unemployment rate.

Two of the biggest wage declines in Table 14, those of 1878 and 1885, were due to national depression-motivated slashes in wage rates. They indicate contra-cyclical employment changes by the firm. The other declines, except for 1893, were modest and occurred because the increased employment made slight changes in the occupational mix. Except for the contra-cyclical hiring in 1878 and 1885, such large employment increases without any wage rate increases indicates a real weakness in the labor market as a force for raising wages. For most years the McCormick Works employment moved in the same direction as the national trend.

For the period since 1899, (3), Table 14, gives the national labor market situation. If it can be assumed that the Chicago labor market resembled the national one, these figures on national unemployment data further the impression of the weakness of labor market forces for raising wages in peacetime years. In the boom years of 1907 and 1926, despite the acute labor shortages revealed by the non-farm unemployment percentages of 2.9 and 2.8 per cent, the McCormick Works increased its work force 15 per cent and 60 per cent without raising wages. The larger relative number of below-average-wage hirees even cut slightly the plant average hourly earnings in those years. Note that the spectacular 1926 employment increase without a wage increase occurred after the curtailment of immigration. The most recent year in which average hourly earnings declines and employment increases occurred simultaneously was 1933. This is because since that date union influence has not only eliminated wage cuts but by bargaining pressure and long-term contracts has brought about wage increases in bad years as well as good.

Another striking way to illustrate the weakness of labor market forces

TABLE 14

AHE Declines and Employment Increases, McCormick Works; National Unemployment

Year	Annual per cent change in AHE (money) McCormick Works	Annual per cent employment change McCormick Works	National unemployment as a per cent of non-farm employees
1866	−2	+63	—ᵃ
1878	−7	+58	—ᵃ
1885	−16	+11	—ᵃ
1893	−7	+17	—ᵃ
1897	−4	+5	—ᵃ
1900	−4	+60	8.7
1905	−0.1	+14	5.1
1907	−2	+15	2.9
1926	−2	+60	2.8
1933	−4	+12	35.3

ᵃ Data not available.

Sources: See sources for (1), (2), and (3) in Appendix B.

on wage change is to examine the variation in wage change and labor market conditions during relatively normal periods of peacetime prosperity.

By removing years of deep depression, Table 15, we can observe the effect on wage change of relatively similar labor market pressures. Column (4), Table 15, indicates that at least for the periods since 1900, labor market forces as measured by unemployment rates were of approximately equal strength. Yet in the relatively prosperous periods listed, money and real average hourly earnings appear quite unrelated either to the firm employment change or to national unemployment trends.

The period of most rapid employment growth for the McCormick Works was 1923–1929 with 9.7 per cent per year. But this was one of the lowest wage increase periods, 0.9 per cent. The 1947–1960 period was one of employment stagnation for the firm, −1.4 per cent per year, and the highest wage gain of any period, 5.8 per cent per year. The average national unemployment rates, (4), Table 15, were identical in both periods. Thus the labor market data fail to provide any explanation of the wide swings of wage change in periods of peacetime prosperity.

What is the possibility that labor market conditions may have caused some of the differing rates of wage change which in Chapter 2 were attributed to trade unionism? Some writers have suggested that not unionism but the end of immigration might have tightened labor market

TABLE 15

Summary of Employment and Earnings Changes, and National Labor Market Conditions during Periods of Peacetime Prosperity

Period	Annual percentage rates of growth, McCormick Works AHE (1)	Annual percentage rates of growth, McCormick Works real AHE (2)	Annual percentage rates of growth, McCormick Works employment (3)	Unemployment as a per cent of non-farm employees (4)
1865–1873	2.4[a]	6.8	3.1	—[b]
1880–1887	0.0	1.4	7.9	—[b]
1887–1893	−2.0	−1.2	0.7	—[b]
1900–1913	1.9	0.7	4.3	6.7
1923–1929	0.9	0.9	9.7	5.5
1947–1960	5.8	3.6	−1.4[c]	5.5
Secular Trend 1860–1960	*2.9*	*2.0*	*3.4*	

[a] Refer to Table 1 for definitions of growth rates, SE, and R^2.
[b] Data not available.
[c] Since the McCormick Works became obsolete during this period, employment in the firm has been substituted in this period for employment at the McCormick Works.

Sources: (1), (2), and (3), Wage and employment data, 1865–1913, from McCormick Works payroll books, in McCormick Collection; 1923–1960, I.H.Co. files, Chicago. For adjustment of fringe benefits in (1), (2) for McCormick Works see sources for (3) in Appendix A.

(4), Unemployment figures 1900–1958, William G. Bowen, *Wage Behavior in the Post-War Period* (Princeton, N.J.: Princeton University Press, 1960), pp. 100–101; 1958–1960, *Economic Report of the President, 1963*, Employment, Wages and Productivity, Table C-19, p. 194.

conditions and accounted for the higher rates of wage change in recent years. In order to examine this proposition it is necessary to select some reasonably comparable time periods both before and after the curtailment of immigration. If we select the periods of prosperity since 1900 we can compare rates of wage changes with labor market conditions as represented by national average rates of unemployment as a per cent of the non-farm population. Table 16 gives facts for the evaluation of this proposition. Note that real wage rates have been used for Table 16 to remove the influence of inflation.

The unemployment and wage change comparisons (Table 16) of the non-depression peacetime years since 1900 lend no support to the hypothesis that the tightening labor market caused by curtailment of immigration was responsible for the higher rate of wage increases in recent years. Although immigration was curtailed as early as 1915, the 1923–1929 period shows no increase in the real rate of wage increase. The biggest real wage increases except for the inflation of 1919–1920 came in the 1935–1941 period, just when the labor market was the loosest. The high rate of real wage increase, 3.6 per cent in the 1947–1960 period at McCormick, occurred with unemployment figures not significantly different from those of 1900–1903, 1905–1907, and 1909–1913, which had an average rate of real wage increase of 1.0 per cent.

The 1919–1920 period, with a high rate of real wage growth and a low rate of unemployment, makes the best case for labor market demand forces as a cause of high wage growth. Immigration had been severely restricted by war since 1915 so that even the renewed flow in 1920 could not make up for the losses of the wartime years. Unfortunately, market demand forces in 1919–1920 cannot be isolated from the concurrent enormous increase in union membership and strike activity. Union membership doubled between 1915 and 1920, most of the increase occurring in 1919 and 1920. More important, 1919 was the country's all-time strike record, surpassing in the per cent of employed workers involved, 20.8 per cent, even the huge strike years of 1946, 14.5 per cent, 1945, 12.2 per cent, and 1937, 7.2 per cent.[2] Of this period it can only be said that a combination of a tight labor market and rapid union growth brought wage increases large enough to overcome the expected wage lag of a rapid inflation.

The collapse of wage growth rates during the prosperity of 1923–1929 indicates that market demand forces were weak as a cause of wage growth. The subsequent explosion of wage growth rates 1935–1941 and

TABLE 16

Immigration, Rates of Wage Change, Levels of Unemployment and Unionization in Prosperous Years

Period	Annual percentage rates of growth, real AHE McCormick Works (1)	Annual percentage rates of growth, real AHE in U.S. manufacturing (2)	Average unemployment as a per cent of non-farm employees (3)	Average unionization as a per cent of the non-farm employees (4)
PROSPEROUS YEARS OF UNRESTRICTED IMMIGRATION				
1900–1903	2.8[a]	2.5	7.5	9.9
1905–1907	−2.7	2.8	3.1	9.8
1909–1913	1.5	1.4	8.2	9.4
Weighted Arithmetic Average	*1.0*	*2.1*	*6.8*	*9.7*
PROSPEROUS YEARS OF RESTRICTED IMMIGRATION				
1919–1920	5.1	5.4	4.6	16.0
1923–1929	0.9	1.1	5.5	11.4
1935–1941	5.0	3.9	22.3	18.7
1947–1960	3.6	3.3	5.5	33.4
Weighted Arithmetic Average	*3.4*	*3.0*	*9.3*	*24.3*
Secular Trend 1860–1960	*2.0[b]*	*2.2*		

[a] 1900–1903 period for McCormick AHE includes January, 1904, to reflect the wage raise which had been agreed to in the union contract of May, 1903.
[b] Refer to Table 1 for definitions of growth rates.

Sources: (1), (2), (3), see sources for (1) and (2) in Appendix A. See sources for (3) in Appendix B.

(4), Union membership data, 1900–1956, U.S. Bureau of the Census, *Historical Statistics, Colonial Times to 1957* (Washington, D.C.: GPO, 1960), pp. 97–98; union membership, 1957–1960, *Monthly Labor Review*, 87 (May, 1964): 504.

1947–1960 when labor market surpluses were general indicates that some other forces counteracted market demand.

The degree of unionization in the periods listed in Table 16 appears more closely associated with rates of wage change than is the level of unemployment. The influence of unionism has two facets; first, level of union membership; and, secondly, the rate of growth of unionism. The high wage growth rate indicated for the 1935–1941 period in Table 16, a period when unemployment was particularly high, must be attributed to the rapid unionization accompanying the organization of the CIO. As the percentage organized reaches its practical potential, somewhere between 30 and 35 per cent of the work force, the growth of unionism declines as a wage influencing variable and is replaced by the bargaining effect of a highly unionized work force.

It would appear from Table 17 (though with several exceptions) that since 1873 the company has become increasingly reluctant to cut wages

TABLE 17

McCormick Works Wage Response Following Downturns in General Business Activity

Year	Date of general business downturn (1)	Date of first wage cut (2)	Lag in months before wage cut (3)
1873	September, 1873	September, 1873	0
1884	May, 1884	December, 1884	7
1893	May, 1893	January, 1894	8[a]
		November, 1896	41[b]
1903–1904	March, 1903	October, 1904	18[c]
1907	August,1907	January, 1908	5
1920	May, 1920	April, 1921	11
1929	October, 1929	November, 1931	25
1937	September, 1937	No cut	—
1948	December, 1948	No cut	—
1953	August, 1953	No cut	—
1957	August, 1957	No cut	—

[a] Skilled.
[b] Common labor.
[c] Delay due to 18-month union contract.

Sources: (1), Hearings Before the Joint Economic Committee of the Congress of the United States, 86 Cong., 1 sess., Part 2, *Historical and Comparative Rates of Production, Productivity, and Prices* (1959), p. 398.

(2), (3), Payroll records Mc.H.M.Co. and I.H.Co., McCormick Collection.
(3), computation by author from data in (1), (2).

when an economic downturn appears. The chief, but not the only reason for this may well have been unionism. In 1873 the company cut wages promptly and suffered a foundry strike. In 1884 the company delayed seven months before cutting wages. A strike occurred anyway and the company was forced to capitulate by restoring the cut. In the depression of 1893 the company, mindful of the 1884–1885 experience, avoided any across-the-board cut and reduced wages of skilled and semi-skilled only. This was clearly an effort to avoid a strike and the accompanying public disfavor. After the 1903 recession began, the com-

TABLE 18

Sales and Profits, International Harvester, 1920–1922, and 1929–1933

Year	Sales (millions)	Per cent change	Profits (millions)	Per cent change
1920	$225.0		$16.6	
1921	121.2	−46.13	4.1	−75.3
1922	132.3	9.16	5.5	+34.15
. . . .	. . .	. . .	. . .	. . .
1929	336.5		36.8	
1930	279.9	−16.82	25.7	−30.16
1931	168.2	−39.9	1.3	−99.49
1932	89.0	−47.09	−7.6	−68.5
1933	93.5	+5.06	−1.9	+75.0

Source: I.H.Co. Offices, Chicago.

pany not only did not cut wages but raised them due to a strike. Later, at the expiration of the union contract in October, 1904, wages were cut after a survey revealed that the union was too weak to strike. In 1907 the wage cut came after only five months, thus constituting an exception to the growing lag in wage cuts; the money panic may have caused the recession to hit more quickly than in earlier downturns. By contrast with the 1903–1904 lag, the 1907 figures show clearly that the effect of product market and labor market conditions are manifest only when unions have been destroyed. In the depression of 1914–1916 wage rates were maintained but weekly hours were cut in some departments in order to divide the work. This, however, was a partial cause of the 1916 strike. In the rapid and severe depression of 1920 the company, despite sharp price and sales declines, waited eleven months before cutting wages. When unemployment became severe enough, it felt safe to institute the cuts. The long delay after the 1929 crash seems indicative of a conscious policy to avoid wage cuts if at all possible. The gradual nature of the 1929–1933 decline in contrast with the speed of the 1920–1922 crash probably accounts for the longer delay in making cuts in the latter depression. Table 18 indicates the sharpness of the 1920–1921 profit decline in comparison to the more gradual decline after 1929.

Since the advent of strong industrial unions on a national scale there have been no wage cuts whatsoever at a McCormick plant despite depressions in 1937, 1949, 1954, and 1958. The very existence of long-term contracts is an admission that wage cuts are a thing of the past for healthy firms.

Though the depressions since the advent of strong national unions have not been so severe as those after 1873, 1893, 1920, or 1929, the depressions of 1937, 1949, 1954, and 1958 have been comparable in severity to those of 1884, 1904, and 1907, all of which resulted in wage cuts at the McCormick Works. The 1904 cut did not occur until the expiration of the union contract.

When wage rates were not slashed in depressions the average hourly earnings rose slightly. This was due to dropping the less skilled and lower paid workers. This occurred in 1914, 1915, 1930, and 1931. In 1905, 1908, and 1932 wage rates had actually been cut but average hourly earnings did not decline as much as might have been expected apparently because the piece workers speeded up their pace and made up for some of the cut.

The growing reluctance of the Harvester Company to cut wages in depressions has stemmed not only from the rigidity of a fixed-term union contract such as 1903–1904, 1949, 1954, and 1958, but at times from the threat of unionism and perhaps from the recognition of its disruptive effect on employee morale. In addition, the long delay after 1929 was due to the gradual onset of the depression.

Upward market demand pressures showed up most clearly in war-time – the Civil War, World War I, World War II, and the Korean War. However, in each of these periods there was militant unionism among McCormick Works employees and the two forces – market demand for labor and unionism – were inextricably commingled. In studying the correspondence of the company executives during the Civil War and World War II, it is clear that many of the major wage movements were made in response to expected labor troubles or to actual strikes – six in the Civil War and two in the World War I period. Wage movements in World War II were controlled by the government. The popular notion that real wages lag during wartime inflation has never been true for McCormick Works employees who, in fact, made real wage gains in every war including the Civil War.

Unionism and market demand for labor are obviously separate forces which frequently function independently of each other. Yet when they function together as in wartime they may have more impact than the sums of their separate strengths.

What would market demand in wartime inflation do to wages in the absence of unionism? There has never been such a period at the McCormick Works. However, if we look at the national wage averages for manufacturing compiled by Long and reproduced on Chart 1 and Table 1, it appears that in the Civil War the upward wage movement was substantially less than at the McCormick Works and that workers nationally suffered substantial real wage losses. If we assume that the manufacturing firms nationally were less unionized than the McCormick Works, we might describe the Civil War U.S. manufacturing wage behavior as more closely responding to market demand. However, the McCormick Works was by no means the only unionized plant and therefore it must be assumed that the market demand by itself would have raised wages even less rapidly than actually occurred. In World War I unionism and market demand were both strong forces reacting on each other and both must share responsibility for the result. Historically market demand has been an important force on wages but, except for wartime at the McCormick Works, it seems to have exerted primarily a downward pressure on wages. After 1873 there appears to have been an almost steady surplus of unskilled labor and often of skilled labor. Pattern shop rates at McCormick's declined between 1888 and 1897 (see Profile 6). Molders' wages dropped from 1887 to 1900.

During peacetime market demand appears almost always to have been a very weak upward force. The enormous employment pick-up of 1899–1902 scarcely budged McCormick wages. When the threat of a union became a reality in late 1902, 1903, and 1904, wages shot up even after the firm's employment had begun to sag with the 1903–1904 depression. Clearly in this period unionism was a more potent force for wage buoyancy than market demand for labor.

Market demand was a major factor in raising skilled rates as exemplified by the McCormick patternmakers from 1906 through 1912 (see Profile 7). Yet during these years union rates in metal trades as compiled by Douglas[4] were substantially higher than Harvester rates so that even here a second factor in the Harvester skilled rate increase of 1906–1912 was the competitive pressure of union rates in other plants.

The International Harvester Company correspondence complained of peacetime labor shortages in 1912, 1923, and 1926. In May of 1912, selected skilled workers were given wage raises of 2.5 cents per hour. This increase was due to skilled labor shortages. On October 1, however, a much broader general increase was given. Hours were cut from 58.5 per week to 55, accompanied by a general increase. Because wage averages for these years were taken as of the first week of April, the 1912 raises of 10 per cent do not show up until 1913 in Appendix B. This general pay raise and cut in hours was not caused by labor shortages, but was made necessary by the company's involvement in the presidential campaign of 1912 through an investigation of working conditions for women at one of the company's twine mills.

In only one instance in the 102-year Harvester wage study was market demand perhaps primarily on its own strength able to bring about a general peacetime wage increase. This occurred in February, 1923. At this time the shortage of skilled labor was enough more acute than the shortage of common labor that skilled labor received a 15 per cent raise to 10 per cent for common labor. In addition, both prior to and after the general increase of February, 1923, special increases were granted to skilled departments to alleviate the shortage. But from May, 1923, throughout the rest of the twenties there were no more increases for either skilled, semi-skilled, or common labor. In the absence of unions the total period of the twenties was characterized by relative wage stability and market demand for labor was revealed as a feeble force by comparison with union pressures of earlier and later periods.

The 1926 labor shortage of skilled workers was met by promotion from the less skilled men within the plant rather than by granting wage increases to existing skilled workers or hiring new employees at top rates. Apparently, except in wartime, labor stringencies never became acute enough to raise wages significantly.

During World War I and during the 1920's the company tried a variety of methods to cope with labor shortages and still limit wage increases. In 1918 and in 1923 the company was faced with a shortage of girls for its Chicago twine mills. The first response was to drop the age limit from 18 to 16 years and then to 14. A second response was to greatly increase the employment of Negroes. A third response was to hire a limited number of men at higher wage rates. This was an economy, because hiring men for a few vacancies was cheaper than raising all the women's wages enough to attract those needed. A fourth method was to leave some machines idle rather than to raise all wages enough to man them. On the basis of long experience, Harvester management viewed a tight labor market as an aberration. It therefore chose to make temporary sacrifices of production rather than to make costly general wage increases which it could not easily cut without bringing on strikes and unions.

By contrast, union demands presented the company with a likelihood of a total withdrawal of labor and a complete cessation of production. Such a threat could be avoided only by substantial general wage increases which, of course, had a much greater impact on wage costs than the piecemeal adjustments called for by labor market shortages.

Another method by which the company attempted to evade the wage impact of market demand forces for labor was by the adoption of monopsonistic practices in the hiring of labor. As early as 1863 the proprietors of iron foundries west of Buffalo met in Chicago to agree on maximum wage rates for molders. In the early periods employers got together informally and agreed on common labor rates and wage cuts in times of recessions. By 1900 such organizations as the National Metal Trades Association and the National Founders Association brought employers together to agree on common wage and hours policies and to oppose union demands. In the 1920's the International Harvester Company joined local groups such as a neighborhood group of employers known as the Chicago Southwest Side Employers. These employers in the neighborhood of the McCormick and Tractor Works met periodically to compare labor market conditions and to avoid competitive wage practices. Nationally the International Harvester Company was a member of the influential Special Conference Committee. These large employers met regularly from 1919 on and exchanged wage and labor relations information. These exchanges appear to have exerted at least some influence toward restraining wage increases in the twenties, and toward delaying wage cuts on the downswing after 1929.

This propensity of employers to establish monopsonistic practices to prevent either unions or the normal market forces from raising wages has been extremely widespread in American industry and of long duration, originating even before the agricultural implement industry was begun. Robert Layer, in a study of early New England cotton mill wage practices, found that in 1834 area cotton mill managers got together to adopt uniform wage policies. Even during the embryo period of American manufacturing, 1832–1860, Mr. Layer declares, "With respect to the data concerning wages, . . . a considerable body of material exists in the company records relating to management's response to the efforts made by employees at labor organization, and attesting to the effectiveness with which the managements of the various companies communicated or combined to prevent competition among them for employees." [5] During the Civil War immigrants were brought in under long-term wage contracts. Anti-piracy agreements and uniform wage increases were common practices. In the seventies, according to Layer, the Fall River textile companies used an industry-wide lockout to block a union demand for wage increases. On December 26, 1883, a 10 per cent wage cut was simultaneously put into effect by ". . . nearly all the companies in New England." [6]

The most important shortcoming of the market demand explanation of wage movements is the dramatic and sustained rise in the rates of wage increase, both money and real, which occurred from 1933 through 1960. Real wages at the McCormick Works rose an average of 2.9 per cent per year from 1933 to 1960, and 3.6 per cent from 1947 to 1960. This is far more than in any of the earlier non-union periods. Since this period was on the whole not characterized by a tighter labor market than earlier periods, some explanation is indicated. The 1933–1960 period has been clearly the most unionized period in the history of the country. The phenomenon of regular annual wage changes appears to be the dominant feature of the high rate of wage increases in this period. The quarterly escalator changes of the 1950's likewise point out the major influence of unionism rather than market demand in this period.

The only period showing sustained wage rate increases comparable to the post-1933 period is the period 1862–1887. Since this period is the only other prolonged period of unionism in the McCormick Works, unionism must be given careful consideration as a major causal factor in wage variation over the 102-year period.

Concurrently with the unionization of the economy after 1933 came an increased role for government. The NRA, the Fair Labor Standards Act of 1938, the government encouragement of unions, have been factors encouraging wage increases during periods of weak market demand. The rigid government wage controls in World War II and the less rigid control in the Korean War temporarily dampened wage raises below what the market and union bargaining power would have achieved.

In spite of management responses designed to avoid the upward pressures of labor shortages, sustained labor shortages of sufficient magnitude would undoubtedly have raised money and even real wages substantially. It is the conclusion of this study, however, that the American economy in peacetime prior to 1964 has not experienced labor shortages of such magnitude. At the McCormick Works market demand for labor in the absence of strong unionism has been accompanied in periods of peacetime prosperity by annual real wage advances averaging about .1 of 1 per cent per year for the 20 such years studied (Table 9). In the presence of unionism in periods of peacetime prosperity there have occurred sustained annual real wage and fringe advances averaging 3.9 per cent for the 31 such years studied (Table 9).

The Wage Rigidity Hypothesis

The growing rigidity of wages during deflation has been illustrated in Table 14. This is a modification of labor market behavior which one might expect with growing unionism. Surprisingly it is alleged by certain wage theorists that there is also a union-caused rigidity during inflation. Albert Rees writes, "In periods of rapid and unexpected inflation, such as occurred from 1941 to 1948, even the strongest unions seem to have no effect on relative earnings or to lose most of any effect they previously had."[7] The rationale behind such loss of union wage impact is explained by Mr. Rees as follows: "During rapid inflations, demand forces pull up product prices and wage rates in non-union markets. Agreements fixing wages for a period of time, or even long-term agreements providing for periodic wage increases according to some pre-agreed formula or schedule can leave unions at a relative disadvantage. The presence of a union, with its power to resist wage cuts at a later date can also dissuage employers from using wage increases to deal with temporary labor shortages."[8] H. Gregg Lewis, studying the period 1920–1958, found union influence on wages highest in 1932 and lowest in the 1947–1948 inflation.[9]

The years chosen by Rees and Lewis, 1941 to 1948, to illustrate the decline of union influence during inflation are not well suited to their purpose because in addition to the inflation effect they include a period of government controls established to put an end to union bargaining power for the duration of the war. In contrast to the view of the ineffectiveness of unions during inflation there is the War Labor Board view that modern union bargaining is so powerful during wartime that it cannot be tolerated. Even after the close of hostilities in 1945 the continuance of federal price controls into 1947 and the general big industry practice of pricing products below free market levels introduced strong forces exerting restraint on wage increases in addition to the effects of the unionism and the inflation variables.

TABLE 19

Peacetime Trough to Peak Wage and Price Changes, Union vs. Non-union Periods, McCormick Works

Trough to peak periods	Growth rates, cost-of-living[a] (1)	Growth rates, McCormick Works real AHE[b] (2)	Growth rates U.S. manufacturing real AHE (3)
UNION			
1879–1883	− .2	7.6	3.2
1885–1887	− .6	10.2	3.5
1900–1903	1.5	2.8[c]	2.5
1933–1937[d]	2.6	6.3	5.0
1954–1957	1.3	3.5	3.3
1958–1960	1.1	4.7	2.9
Weighted Arithmetic Average 18 union years	1.1	5.9	3.5
NON-UNION			
1891–1893	−1.1	0.1	3.7
1905–1907	2.8	−2.7	2.8
1908–1913	1.6	1.1	1.4
1922–1926	1.3	2.1	1.3
Weighted Arithmetic Average 13 non-union years	1.3	0.7	1.9
Secular Trend 1890–1960		2.0	

[a] Annual averages of each year except 1954–1957, 1958–1960, and 1926, where April cost-of-living figures are used to correspond with April wage data in (2).
[b] April data for all years except 1922–1925, where only annual averages were used, and 1903, where January, 1904, was the wage peak.
[c] Includes wage increases agreed to in union contract of May, 1903, but not put into effect till January, 1904.
[d] No outside unions at McCormick Works, but rapid union growth nationally.

Sources: See sources for (1), (2), (3), (4) in Table 1.

The hundred-year wage movement at the McCormick Works gives no support to the Friedman-Lewis-Rees [10] wage rigidity-during-inflation hypothesis. In the first place there has been so little peacetime inflation in the United States since 1860 that it is very difficult to observe the reaction of wages during inflation. Table 19 (p. 99) compares real wage changes and cost-of-living movements from business cycle troughs to prosperity peaks during both union and non-union periods.

From (2), Table 19, it is clear that in the typically mild inflations accompanying business recovery in peacetime, real wages in the unionized periods were substantially less rigid — rising 5.9 per cent per year — than in the non-union periods when real wages rose on the average 0.7 per cent annually. For U.S. manufacturing — (3), Table 19 — for the depressions selected the findings point in the same direction. The conclusions for U.S. manufacturing are less valid, however, because the difference in the amount of unionism in the "union" and "non-union" periods is a matter of degree rather than the clear-cut "union" or "non-union" condition at the McCormick Works. For example, in manufacturing the highest wage growth rate of the non-union period — 3.7 per cent from 1891 to 1893 — could be partially explained by the greater degree of unionism in "manufacturing" than in the "McCormick Works" which was still suffering from the complete abolition of unions as a result of the union defeat in the strikes of 1886. Nevertheless, the amount and strength of unionism in the so-called "union" years for U.S. manufacturing was significantly greater than in the non-union years (or rather, years of weak unionism).

It is, of course, clear that this entire comparison of Table 19 suffers from the fact that the strength of market demand for labor was not equal in the various trough to peak periods listed above. The "union" periods contain recovery from two very serious depressions, those of the 1870's and the 1930's. But the union period also contains recovery from two depression periods, 1954 and 1958, in which there were wage increases instead of cuts.

The point of Table 19 is that there is absolutely no historical evidence pointing to greater wage flexibility on the upswing from depressions during non-union or weak union periods. Rather, what evidence there is points in the other direction. Column (2), which covers the clear-cut union vs. non-union wage behavior at the McCormick Works, emphatically supports the greater flexibility on the upswing of the periods when the McCormick Works was unionized.

TABLE 20

Rate of Inflation, Real Changes, in AHE, and Union Status, Four Wars

Wartime inflationary periods	Growth rates C.P.I.[a] (1)	Growth rates real AHE McCormick Works[b] (2)	Union status[c] (3)
		McCormick Works	
1861–1865	16.8[d]	4.7	Strong union but no written contract.
1915–1920	15.2	5.4	Unions not recognized but a constant threat, major strikes in McCormick Works 1916 and 1919.
1940–1948	6.3	1.5	Strong unions, written contracts, 1942–1948.
1950–1953	3.9[e]	4.5[e]	Strong unions, written contracts.
		U.S. Manufacturing[d]	
(Annual Averages)			
1861–1865	16.8[d]	−7.4	Weakest unionism of the four periods.
1915–1920	15.2	4.8	Rapidly growing unions. 1919 greatest strike year in U.S. history.
1940–1948	6.6	2.5	Strong and growing unionism. 1946 second greatest strike year in U.S. history.
1949–1953	3.4	4.1	Strongest union period. Highest proportion of work force under union.

[a] CPI data are annual data except for the McCormick Works years 1940–1953 where April data are used to correspond with the April data of the McCormick Works. June, 1948, replaces April, 1948.
[b] Wage data are April data for the McCormick Works except for (a) 1915–1920, where annual averages are used and (b) June, 1948, replaces April, 1948.
[c] Union status is based on judgment of author.
[d] Refer to Table 1 for definitions of growth rates.
[e] Since McCormick Works wages for this period are April figures, the years 1950–1953 encompass the wage changes of the Korean War; U.S. manufacturing wages, however, are annual data. Therefore to avoid including the war-influenced wage raises of the second half of 1950 it was necessary to revert back to 1949, the last year uninfluenced by the war.

Sources: (1), see sources for (2), Table 1.
         (2), Appendix A.

The biggest inflationary periods since 1860 have been the war periods and in the case of World Wars I and II the years immediately after the close of hostilities. Table 20 gives comparative data on inflation, real wage gains, and union status in wartime inflation for both U.S. manufacturing and for the McCormick Works.

On their face the data in Table 20 are somewhat contradictory in relation to the viewpoint that unionism loses its wage impact during rapid inflationary periods. There have only been four brief inflationary periods, all wartime phenomena, since the rise of U.S. manufacturing: the Civil War, 1861–1865; World War I and its aftermath, 1915–1920; World War II and its aftermath, 1940–1948; and the Korean War, 1950–1953. So far as U.S. manufacturing is concerned, Table 20 indicates that the greatest wage rigidity in these inflationary periods occurred in the least unionized period, 1861–1865, with a real AHE rate of −7.4 per cent (see [2], Table 20). By contrast, the unionized McCormick Works in this same Civil War period showed greater upward wage flexibility, real AHE rate of 4.7 per cent (see [2], Table 20), than the less unionized U.S. manufacturing average.

The evidence on any tendencies toward wage rigidity in non-unionized inflationary periods is even more limited at the McCormick Works than for U.S. manufacturing. The McCormick Works was unionized during the Civil War so there is no opportunity to observe wage behavior in inflation not influenced by unions. The Civil War unionism at the McCormick Works resulted merely in verbal wage agreements of no set time duration. Unions were therefore free to negotiate and strike whenever they wished and were not restricted to long-term contracts. In the World War I period International Harvester did not recognize outside unions, but prolonged strikes in its major Chicago plants (including the McCormick Works) in 1916 and 1919 plus the rapid growth of unions and the huge strike wave of 1919 contributed greatly to wage flexibility.

The evidence supporting the view of unionism as a cause of rigidity in inflation is limited to the one period, 1940–1948, when the real wage increase was the least of the four wartime periods (Table 20). However, as already mentioned, much of this period should be discounted due to government restrictions on collective bargaining from 1942 through at least 1946. Even after the end of price control in 1947, the threat of a reimposition of price controls encouraged employers to resist cost-raising wage increases. In April, 1947, International Harvester, in a sincere but hopeless cause, purchased full-page newspaper ads to announce to the public a substantial price rollback on its products. Agricultural implement, auto, and steel industries marketed their products at prices well below the free market levels in efforts to avoid public and customer censure and to retard inflation. In 1948 big industry attempted a wage freeze to stop inflation. Strikes in Chrysler and threats of strikes in other industries plus the continuing rise of prices finally broke the freeze and set in motion the third round of post-war wage increases. From the end of the war in 1945 through 1948 not unionism but determined government and public opposition to inflation spurred industry to resist union wage demands which it was reluctant to follow with compensating price increases.

The view that unions retarded wage increases during the 1945–1948 inflation seems to rest upon the following doubtful assumptions:

a. that in the absence of unions there would have existed a labor market relatively free of monopsony;
b. that a free labor market from 1945 to 1948 would have called for wages above the then existing union-management negotiated rates for prime employers;
c. that employers from 1945 to 1948 tolerated substantial labor shortages rather than reopen their union contracts prior to the annual reopening date in the agreement.

An examination of labor market conditions in the inflationary years, 1945–1948, does not indicate that free market forces would have pushed wages higher or even as high as they went under union bargaining. Table 21 compares unemployment, quit rates, and money wage changes for the non-union twenties with the 1945–1949 period and the Korean War period.

From (1) and (2) of Table 21 it appears that labor market conditions were no tighter in the inflationary post-war forties and early fifties than in the stable twenties. If we discount the quit rates of 1945 and 1946 as due to wartime and reconversion, the quit rates of the latter period were generally lower than in the wage stable twenties. Specifically the quit and unemployment rates of 1929, identical to those of 1947, did not produce rapidly rising wages in the non-union conditions of 1929. On balance, it is difficult to see in the labor market figures of the post-World War II period any forces that would have generated substantial wage increases without the aid of union bargaining. The steadily declining quit rates after 1945 from 5.1 to 2.8 in 1948 indicate that perhaps the cancellation of war contracts and the returning servicemen supplied a reservoir of labor which was a restraining force on wages despite the rapid inflation in the latter part of 1946 and 1947. Thus it was apparently the cost-of-living changes and the strong unionism rather than the labor market situation which provided the upward wage push of the post-World War II period. This gives no support to the wage-rigidity hypothesis of Friedman, Lewis, and Rees.

During the Korean War government wage controls again curtailed

TABLE 21

Labor Market Conditions: Quit Rates, Unemployment, Wage and Cost-of-Living Changes, 1923–1930 and 1945–1953

Year	Quit rates in U.S. manufacturing (monthly average) (1)	Unemployment as a per cent of non-farm work force (2)	AHE U.S. manufacturing percentage changes over previous year (3)	Cost-of-living percentage changes over previous year (4)
1923	6.2	4.6	6.3	1.8
1924	2.7	8.0	4.8	0.3
1925	3.1	5.9	0.0	2.0
1926	2.9	2.8	0.2	1.3
1927	2.1	5.9	0.4	−0.6
1928	2.2	6.4	2.2	−2.9
1929	3.4	4.7	0.7	0.0
1930	1.6	13.0	−2.5	−1.3
. . . .	.	.	.	.
1945	5.1	2.5	1.0	1.9
1946	4.3	5.2	6.6	3.2
1947	3.4	4.7	15.0	19.2
1948	2.8	4.5	8.5	8.4
1949	1.5	7.3	3.5	0.2
1950	1.9	6.6	6.2	−0.7
1951	2.4	3.8	11.6	9.6
1952	2.3	3.4	5.8	2.3
1953	2.3	3.2	6.0	0.7

Sources: (1), U.S. Bureau of the Census, *Historical Statistics, Colonial Times to 1957* (Washington, D.C.: GPO, 1960), p. 100.

(2), Wm. G. Bowen, *Wage Behavior in the Post-War Period* (Princeton, N.J.: Princeton University Press, 1960), pp. 100–101.

(3), 4), see Table 1.

TABLE 22

United States Unemployment as a Per Cent of Civilian Labor
Force and the Chicago Labor Market, 1945–1953[a]

Year	United States (1)	Chicago labor market (2)
1945	1.9	3.4
1946	3.9	5.0
1947	3.6	3.4
1948	3.4	3.5
1949	5.5	6.0
1950[b]	5.0	4.7
1951[b]	3.0	2.6
1952	2.7	2.5
1953	2.5	1.9

[a] Annual averages.

[b] Assumes March 15, 1950, and 1951 figures as the annual averages.

Sources: (1), U.S. Bureau of the Census, *Historical Statistics, Colonial Times to 1957* (Washington, D.C.: GPO, 1960), Series D 46–47, p. 73.

(2), Illinois Department of Labor, Division of Research and Statistics, Unemployment and labor force estimates (from 1945 to 1948) for Illinois section of Chicago, Calumet labor market area, and includes Cook and De Pere counties. 1949 labor force data are the average of 1948 annual figures and March 15, 1950.

union bargaining power. The low quit rates of 1951–1953 in the presence of low unemployment rates indicate a probable secular decline due to seniority and pensions.

Table 22 merely indicates that the Chicago labor market 1945–1948 did not differ appreciably from the national market except that 1945 and 1946 showed somewhat more unemployment. By 1952 and 1953 the Chicago labor market was a bit tighter but in these years the low quit rates (Tables 21 and 23) indicate that there was little upward wage pressure from the labor market side.

So far as the labor market situation in International Harvester was concerned, company officials report that there was no labor shortage after the end of World War II.[11] Cancellation of war contracts and returning veterans furnished an ample labor supply to the company. It took a sixty-day strike in the spring of 1946 for the unions to get the 18-cent wage increase pattern for that year. The settlement provided for a 10 per cent increase retroactive to October 1, 1945, so that the delay in settlement did not result in wage rigidity during this period. Additional strikes were required to reach pattern settlements in 1947 and

1948. In the light of the ample supply of labor at International Harvester from 1945 to 1948 and the strikes at contract settlements, it is extremely difficult to believe that the company would have raised its wages more in the absence of unions.

An examination of International Harvester's annual Labor Market Summaries[12] for the years 1945 through 1949 and for the Korean War period revealed complaints of labor shortage only prior to October,

TABLE 23

Quit Rates, U.S. Manufacturing and International Harvester, 1945–1953

Year	U.S. manufacturing (1)	International Harvester, all plants (2)	International Harvester, six Chicago plants (3)	International Harvester, McCormick Works (4)
1945	5.1	4.2	3.3	3.6
1946	4.3	2.7	2.1	1.9
1947	3.4	2.6	2.4	2.1
1948	2.8	2.5	2.2	1.9
1949	1.5	1.0	0.8	0.5
1950	1.9	1.4	1.3	0.8
1951	2.4	1.5	1.3	0.8
1952	2.3	1.5	1.6	0.7
1953	2.3	1.9	1.7	1.6

Sources: (1), U.S. Bureau of the Census, *Historical Statistics, Colonial Times to 1957* (Washington, D.C.: GPO, 1960), p. 100.

(2), (3), (4), I.H.Co. files, Chicago.

1945. To check further the actual labor market situation in the International Harvester Company, Table 23 was compiled, giving voluntary quit rates for the inflationary periods 1945–1949 and 1950–1953 in the entire company, in the Chicago area as indicated by average quit rates at Harvester's six Chicago plants, and at the McCormick Works.

Table 23 reveals substantially lower quit rates for International Harvester than for U.S. manufacturing. It is, of course, normal for big, relatively high wage firms to have lower quit rates than the national average. The quit rates of roughly 2 per cent for 1946–1948 at the McCormick Works were typical of most Harvester plants. The higher company average was due to special circumstances at several plants unrelated to labor market shortages. In the 1920's quit rates for U.S. manufacturing of 3.4 per cent in 1929 did not raise wages. On the other hand, the quit rate in U.S. manufacturing of 6.2 per cent for 1923 did indicate real labor shortages. But the high 1945 quit rates did not indicate labor shortage since they were influenced by abnormal dislocations due to the ending of the war. There seems no reason to suspect that the Harvester quit rates of the magnitude of 2 to 3 per cent which existed from 1946 to 1948 would have boosted wages in the absence of union pressure. Prime employers in each community such as Harvester already paid wages well above going market wage rates. Labor market pressures, therefore, were probably felt primarily in the low-wage firms.

Quite clearly unionism has two tendencies bearing upon wages in inflationary periods. The stronger tendency is toward wage flexibility as workers made restless by inflation bargain and strike for substantial raises. There is a secondary tendency toward rigidity due to annual contracts which in a fast moving inflation delay the onset of bargaining. Even here, of course, the delay in opening contracts means less rigidity than the absence of unionism. No employer will forego necessary labor merely because his union contract has six months to run. If market forces call for wage increases, the employer will reopen the contract and offer a wage increase rather than curtail operations. If in 1947 and 1948 employers did not reopen contracts it was because they did not have critical labor shortages and hence in the absence of unions would not have raised wages any sooner than the opening of the contract. This analysis does not deny that employers may have relaxed standards on incentive rates and on hiring. However, the large strike waves of 1946–1948 imply that wages in big industry in this period were generally increased due to unionism not to labor market forces.

By contrast, between June and December, 1950, after the Korean War had begun, many employers in anticipation of another wartime labor shortage reopened long duration union contracts and raised wages. During the Korean War cost-of-living escalators gave quarterly adjustments to Harvester wages and curtailed the tendency toward rigidity. In spite of the very low unemployment rates in 1952 and 1953 (Table 23) quit rates nationally and at International Harvester were far lower than in earlier periods of comparably low unemployment. This appears to indicate a secular decline in quit rates due probably to pensions and seniority practices. Since unions have been largely responsible for these practices, unions have to some extent reduced labor mobility which weakens the normal labor market pressures on wage rates. The loss of wage flexibility from this source is probably small compared to the upward wage pressure resulting from union collective bargaining.

6

The Wage Impact of Value Productivity

In addition to the earlier work of Douglas[1] there are two recent empirical studies which report a close linking between total factor productivity and real wage movements.

Albert Rees, comparing manufacturing real wages and factor productivity from 1889 to 1913 found them both growing at an average rate of 1.3 per cent. Rees, however, recognized that rates of both wage increase and productivity rose in subsequent years. He speculates that both the low rates of wage increase and productivity in the 1889–1913 period may have been due to heavy immigration.[2]

If the data from the same sources used by Rees are extended from 1889 to 1957 a quite different conclusion appears. In the longer period total factor productivity rises at the rate of 1.6 per cent per year but real manufacturing wages go up by 2.4 per cent per year.

In Table 24 both long-run and decade-by-decade relationships between total factor productivity and wage growth rates can be compared. A close tie between factor productivity and wage rate movements did not really exist in the decade-by-decade analysis. In certain short periods, particularly when unionism was weak such as the period 1889–1913 reported by Rees, real wage rate growth was as low as productivity. In the periods of strong unionism wage rate growth regularly exceeded productivity.

Solomon Fabricant appears to support a close long-run link between productivity and wages, declaring that, ". . . over the long run the dominant factor in the general rise of real hourly earnings has been the increase in national productivity, and that the more rapid rise in earnings generally than in output per unit of labor and tangible capital combined has resulted largely from greater scarcity of labor relative to capital and from improved quality of labor."[3]

Fabricant sees a definite rise in the rate of productivity advance about 1919 which he further believes is responsible for the higher rate of real wage advances since that date. However, if rates of wage change are studied in Table 24 they do not begin their rise in 1919 but in the mid-1930's. This real wage upturn of the mid-1930's was closely associated with government action and trade unionism rather than with increased productivity. There was a sharp upturn in productivity in manufacturing in the 1920's, 5.2 per cent per year from 1919 to 1929, but it had no apparent effect on real average hourly earnings in manufacturing which rose only 1.6 per cent in the same period.[4]

John W. Kendrick appears to differ from Fabricant on the close relationship between productivity and real average hourly labor compensation. Noting, as had Fabricant, that real average earnings of employees had risen proportionately more than total factor productivity, Kendrick declared that it was theoretically possible for wage rates (or unit capital compensation) to rise faster than total factor productivity over a long period of time so long as the return to the other factor declines. Under such circumstances even the product price can remain stable.[5] Kendrick computed the coefficient of rank correlation of relative changes in output per man hour versus average hourly compensation for eighty manufacturing industries, 1899–1954, and for various sub-periods. The coefficients were positive but barely significant, only .26 for the period.[6] Thus Kendrick, looking at much the same data as Fabricant, sees no close relationship between productivity and average hourly compensation. Kendrick does not offer an explanation of wage rate movements. The differing terminology used by Kendrick and Fabricant would not explain their different conclusions. "Average hourly compensation" as used by Kendrick includes fringe benefits. They were significant only after World War II.

Changes in real net product per capita in the total economy have not historically been limited to rates of total factor productivity change. In Table 24, (1), (2), and (3) indicate that particularly in the years before 1919 increasing amounts of factor input per capita (chiefly capital) accompanied a real net product per capita growth rate in excess of productivity changes.

TABLE 24

Relation of Productivity, Real Net National Product per Capita, and
Wages 1889–1957 and Sub-Periods
(Annual Average Rates of Change)

Period	Total factor productivity[a] (1)	Factor input per capita[a] (2)	Real N.N.P. per capita[a] (3)	Annual percentage rates of growth real AHE U.S. manufacturing (4)	Annual percentage rates of growth real AHE McCormick Works (5)
1889–1957	1.6	0.4	2.0	2.4[b]	2.4[b]
1889–1919	1.4	1.0	2.4	1.5	1.0
1919–1953	1.7	0.1	1.8	3.0	3.1
1889–1913[c]	1.3	—[d]	—[d]	1.3	—[d]
1889–1899	1.5	1.1	2.6	0.8	−0.2
1899–1909	1.1	1.2	2.3	1.4	0.6
1909–1919	1.5	0.8	2.3	2.5	3.1
1919–1929	1.4	0.1	1.6	1.6	1.0
1929–1937	1.1	−1.6	−0.5	3.8	5.1
1937–1948	2.2	1.0	3.2	3.2	1.4
1953–1957	1.5	−1.1	0.4	2.9	2.8

[a] For an understanding of the terms used here and some of their limitations, see: John W. Kendrick, *Productivity Trends in The United States* (Princeton, N.J.: Princeton University Press, 1961), Chapters 1 and 2.

(1), Total factor productivity is a ratio of output to all inputs (both capital and labor) in real terms. The productivity concept is thus one of value productivity not physical productivity.

(2), Factor input per capita is based on labor input per capita and capital input per capita.

(3), Real net national product per capita is based on total factor productivity and factor input per capita.

Calculations for (1), (2), and (3) were simple compound interest formula based on initial and terminal years.

[b] See Table 1 for definitions of growth rate.

[c] The data for this period for (1) and (4) for the period 1889–1913 are from Albert Rees, *Real Wages in Manufacturing, 1890–1914* (Princeton, N.J.: Princeton University Press, 1961), p. 123.

[d] Data not available.

Sources: (1), (2), and (3), Kendrick, *Productivity Trends in the United States*, p. 84.
        (4), (5), see sources for Table 1.

Column (3), Table 24, "Real net national product per capita," indicates that the economy was just as able to support large real wage increases prior to 1919 as it has been since then. In fact, the rate of change (3) from 1899 to 1919 was 2.4 per cent per year compared to only 1.8 per cent since. Thus the historic trends of productivity and real net product per capita do not provide any real answers as to why wage rate changes — (4) and (5) in Table 24 — have varied so much from time to time. These wage trends, both real and money, however, are not inconsistent with the hypothesis of significant trade union impact on wage determination.

In the non-union periods from 1899 to 1929 (skipping the 1909–1919 World War period), productivity gains exceeded real wage gains. In the unionized post-1929 period (skipping World War II) McCormick wage gains have regularly exceeded productivity in the farm equipment industry.

Some productivity information for the McCormick Works is available in the form of labor cost per machine from 1879 to 1894 and is reproduced in Table 26 along with machines manufactured, hourly earnings, and profits.

Table 26 does not give accurate productivity data. However, the

TABLE 25

Productivity, Farm Equipment Industry (except Tractors) and
Real Wage Changes, McCormick Works

Period	Annual average percentage changes in OMH[a] (1)	Annual percentage rates of growth, real wages McCormick Works (2)
1899–1909	+2.5	0.6[b]
1909–1919	−0.4	3.1
1919–1929	+3.5	1.0
1929–1937	+1.0	5.1
1937–1948	+4.3	1.4
1948–1954	0.4	4.1

[a] OMH (output per man hour) refers to constant dollar value of output.
[b] Refer to Table 1 for definitions of growth rates.

Sources: (1), OMH data, John W. Kendrick, *Productivity Trends in the United States* (Princeton, N.J.: Princeton University Press, 1961), p. 486, rates calculated by use of simple compound interest formula.
    (2), see sources for Table 1.

TABLE 26

AHE, Unit Labor Costs, Machines Manufactured, and Profits

Year	Machines manufactured (1)	Labor cost per machine (2)	AHE (3)	Profits (4)
1879	18,758	$14.82	$.162	$ 722,326
1880	21,555	15.07	.187	1,192,733
1881	30,783	17.39	.216	1,254,961
1882	46,687	13.99	.224	1,761,226
1883	48,020	—ª	.212	1,486,632
1884	54,841	—ª	.215	1,776,506
1885	—ª	—ª	.180	841,007
1886	37,712	16.16	.201	679,924
1887	60,221	11.13	.216	1,007,767
1888	76,534	9.77	.208	1,473,986
1889	85,352	8.07	.213	1,803,319
1890	88,114	6.73	.213	1,543,037
1891	111,882	5.59	.192	1,867,058
1892	145,801	5.01	.203	2,550,322
1893	163,011	5.19	.188	2,056,481
1894	119,492	4.71	.182	1,502,581

ª Data not available.

Sources: (1), (2), and (4), from company memoranda, McCormick Collection,
(3) from letters, C. A. Spring to C. H. McC. I, Sept. 27, 1881 (labor cost per machine was $15.065 in 1880 and $17.389 in 1881) and Sept. 18, 1882.

fact that unit labor costs declined after 1887 faster than average hourly earnings implies that productivity was increasing rapidly. The rising profits indicate that market conditions were not such as to pass along the entire productivity increment to the consumer, and that capital rather than unit labor input was capturing the productivity gain.

The productivity data on the McCormick Works is not accurate enough to reach firm conclusions on its influence on wages. What data are contained in Tables 25 and 26 imply that wage changes are not closely related to productivity. Table 25 actually shows a strong inverse relationship. The findings of Tables 25 and 26 lend no support to the hypothesis that changes in productivity are responsible for the differing rates of wage change in either the McCormick Works or in U.S. manufacturing.

The conclusions which come from the data of this chapter do not question the long-run link between total factor productivity plus input of factors and total factor incomes. They do, however, appear to refute the notion that changes in productivity within the ranges that have occurred in this period can account for the changing rates of real wage movements in U.S. manufacturing or at the McCormick Works. The trend at least in the periods 1929–1937, 1937–1948, and 1948–1957 seems further to indicate that one factor — manufacturing real wages — has been rising more rapidly than productivity.

Without some pressure such as unionism, real wage gains could likewise fall below productivity for considerable periods of time or indefinitely. Factor shares are actually constantly changing and even within a factor share such as labor there is room for considerable redistribution of income as among groups of workers.

This variability in returns to labor and capital are illustrated by the following data from Kendrick. In the private domestic economy, labor's share of productivity gains was 81.2 per cent from 1919 to 1929, 135.0 per cent from 1929 to 1937, 69.0 per cent from 1937 to 1948, and 121.8 per cent from 1948 to 1957.[7]

7

The Wage Impact of the Product Market

The product market is a fourth possible wage determinant. John R. Commons attributed the break-up of the early unions in shoemaking to the improved transportation which widened and intensified competition in the product market. This, plus the advent of the merchant-capitalist system of business organization, forced down prices and wages and rendered unions useless because the employer was merely a sweatshop boss with no ability to influence the product market price.

From the time in 1847 when Cyrus H. McCormick established his own reaper factory, he controlled both the manufacture and the sale of the complete product. The enormous growth of the market, and regular price-fixing agreements beginning at least as early as 1863, freed the company for many years from serious product market competition. From 1873 to 1980 the manufacture of agricultural machinery fell into the control of a handful of big producers. In the late nineties through 1901 a brief period of intensive product market competition developed as these rival giants strove for supremacy. The result was that two firms, McCormick and Deering, prospered and increased their share of the market while the others began to lose money. This competitive war resulted in a strong impetus to combination.

The merger of five large competing implement companies into the International Harvester Company was consummated in October, 1902. At birth it produced 85 per cent of the nation's agricultural machinery.[1] At this time even the semblance of price competition ended.

The government won an anti-trust suit against International Harvester in 1917. As a result, the company after World War I was ordered to sell certain lines of its business. This plus the entry of new firms into industry seems to have restored substantial competition by the end of World War II, though a few large firms controlled a large share of the market. The term "oligopoly" would describe the present product market structure.[2]

Table 27 compares profit data with wage changes. Since the product market has only varied between oligopoly and monopoly, profits may be the best index of the varying degrees of departure from competition.

Prior to 1903–1904, cyclical downturns had surprisingly little effect on McCormick Company profits (Table 27). Wages were cut during the downturns beginning in 1873, 1884, and 1893. The reason for wage cutting was more to take advantage of the labor market situation than to respond to severe downward profit pressure. Profit declines in the recession of 1903–1904 did result directly in wage cuts in 1904. The 1907 recession resulted in a small wage cut even though profits on an annual basis rose in both 1907 and 1908. In the severe profit decline of 1913–1915 wages were not cut. This first failure to cut wages in a depression may very likely have been due to the fact that the government's anti-trust suit was then pending in a Minneapolis court. Instead, workers were put on short work weeks. The 1920–1921 and 1929–1932 severe profit declines eventually brought wage cuts though the gradual profit decline after 1929 delayed wage cuts until October, 1931. Clearly, it took more than a protected product market position to block wage cuts. Since 1932 there have been no wage rate cuts at the International Harvester Company.

The profit figures up to 1902 (Table 27) indicate that in the previous history of the McCormick Company downward pressures on wages had not been due to low profits, with the exceptions of the long depression of 1873–1879. Once the International Harvester Trust was formed in 1902 and competition ended, the farmers went on a buying strike. Sales fell; profits for 1903 crashed to only 8.3 per cent of the combined 1902 profits of the former constituent companies. Simultaneously, unionism in the 1903 strike boosted wages. Thus, the almost complete monopolization of the product market was associated with the first serious profit decline. The wage cuts of 1904 stemmed directly from the disappointing profits of the new Harvester trust. Significantly, the cuts could not be instituted until the expiration of the union's contract in September, 1904.

TABLE 27

AHE, Profits and Percentage Changes in AHE, Profits and Net Profits as a Per Cent of Investment, McCormick Harvesting Machine Company and International Harvester

Year	AHE McCormick Works, cents per hour (1)	Per cent change in AHE, if 3 per cent or more (2)	Net profits after taxes Mc.H.M.C., I.H. Co. (3)	I.H. Co. net profits as a per cent of investment[a] (4)
1871	23.3	—[b]	$ 358,894	
1872	22.6	−3.2	—[b]	
1873	26.1	+15.7	—[b]	
1874	23.8	−8.8	276,000	
1875	20.6	−13.5	630,000	
1876	19.8	−4.1	—	
1877	18.5	−6.6	325,000	
1878	17.2	−6.8	618,000	
1879	16.2	−5.8	722,326	
1880	18.7	+15.4	1,192,733	
1881	21.6	+15.2	1,254,961	
1882	22.4	+3.9	1,761,226	
1883	21.2	−5.4	1,486,632	
1884	21.5	−16.3	1,776,506	
1885	18.0	+11.7	841,007	
1886	20.1	+7.5	679,924	
1887	21.6	−3.7	1,007,767	
1888	20.8	—[b]	1,473,986	
1889	21.3	—[b]	1,803,319	
1890	21.3	—[b]	1,543,037	
1891	19.2	−9.9	1,867,058	
1892	20.3	5.5	2,550,322	
1893	18.8	−7.2	2,056,481	
1894	18.2	−3.2	1,502,581	
1895	17.2	−5.5	2,419,978	
1896	18.2	5.8	2,271,184	
1897	17.5	−3.9	2,620,930	
1898	18.3	+4.6	4,799,811	
1899	19.4	+6.0	4,751,828	
1900	18.7	−3.6	4,829,229	
1901	18.9	—[b]	5,185,191	
1902	19.4	—[b]	9,636,629[c]	
1903	20.9	+7.7	796,822[d]	
1904	22.0	+5.3	5,682,445	
1905	21.8	—[b]	7,511,284	
1906	22.2	—[b]	7,406,946	
1907	21.8	—[b]	8,227,716	
1908	22.0	—[b]	10,179,726	

TABLE 27 (continued)

Year	AHE McCormick Works, cents per hour (1)	Per cent change in AHE, if 3 per cent or more (2)	Net profits after taxes Mc.H.M. Co., I.H. Co. (3)	I.H. Co. net profits as a per cent of investment[a] (4)
1909	21.6	—[b]	16,458,843	
1910	22.8	+5.6	17,208,597	
1911	23.8	+4.4	16,638,703	
1912	22.9	—3.8	16,395,597	
1913	25.4	+10.9	7,915,526	
1914	26.2	+3.1	7,463,231	
1915	26.8	—[b]	8,576,435	
1916	29.1	+8.6	10,682,160	
1917	37.5	+28.9	—1,350,722[c]	
1918	47.7	+27.2	14,985,325	
1919	55.5	+16.4	12,608,726	
1920	67.5	+21.6	16,655,353	
1921	66.5	—[b]	4,149,919	
1922	52.2	—21.5	5,540,767	
1923	58.5	+12.3	10,274,377	
1924	61.1	+4.4	13,037,395	
1925	61.5	—[b]	19,171,240	
1926	60.4	—[b]	22,658,892	
1927	60.8	—[b]	23,359,215	
1928	63.2	+3.9	29,685,350	
1929	62.6	—[b]	36,779,998	
1930	63.3	—[b]	25,703,191	
1931	64.2	—[b]	1,346,538	
1932	59.5	—7.3	—7,582,879	
1933	57.1	—4.0	—1,886,257	
1934	61.3	+7.4	3,948,637	
1935	64.6	+5.4	19,618,238	
1936	69.6	+7.7	29,760,372	
1937	82.6	+18.7	32,492,763	
1938	82.6	—[b]	18,471,723	
1939	83.9	—[b]	12,980,059	
1940	84.4	—[b]	23,161,110	
1941	93.5	+10.8	30,634,588	
1942	98.0	+4.8	26,746,552	
1943	108.8	+8.0	25,692,944	
1944	114.7	+8.4	25,396,709	
1945	118.4	+3.2	24,447,210	
1946	125.2	+5.7	22,326,257	
1947	142.4	+13.7	48,469,266	10.63
1948	158.3	+11.2	55,679,337	11.37
1949	170.8	+7.9	61,270,433	11.85

TABLE 27 (continued)

Year	AHE McCormick Works, cents per hour (1)	Per cent change in AHE, if 3 per cent or more (2)	Net profits after taxes Mc.H.M. Co., I.H. Co. (3)	I.H. Co. net profits as a per cent of investment[a] (4)
1950	174.5	—[b]	66,714,716	10.86
1951	202.7	+16.2	63,001,033	9.66
1952	222.3	+9.7	55,656,188	6.15
1953	222.8	—[b]	52,029,417	6.48
1954	221.5	—[b]	36,303,833	4.45
1955	229.3	—[b]	55,501,272	6.58
1956	241.8	+5.5	49,618,709	5.76
1957	258.9	+7.1	45,620,283	5.90
1958	279.5	+8.0	42,987,435	5.50
1959	300.3	+7.4	76,416,279	9.30
1960	313.0	+4.2	53,718,298	5.30

[a] Data not available until 1947.
[b] Not recorded if less than 3 per cent.
[c] Combined profits of the five companies which merged to form I.H.Co.
[d] Profits from 1903 to 1960 are from I.H.Co.
[e] In 1917 I.H.Co. wrote off its wartime loss of property in Russia, Germany, etc., which explains the abnormally low level.

Sources: (1), see sources for Table 1.
(3), see sources for Table 6.
(4), 1947–1956, A. D. H. Kaplan, Joel B. Derlam, and Robert F. Louzillotte, *Pricing in Big Business* (Washington, D.C.: The Brookings Institution, 1958), p. 137; 1957–1960, *Fortune Magazine*, Annual Directory, 1958–1961.

It is very difficult to generalize on the varied relationships of profits and AHE at the McCormick Works. Prior to 1902 the profit trend was rising almost steadily with clearly little relationship to wages. In 1903 a profit decline coincided with a strike-caused wage gain. But at the end of 1904 the sharp profit decline brought a wage cut. At the International Harvester Company only sharp and continued profit declines were reflected in wage cuts. The growing profits of 1909 and 1910 had little effect on wages. The substantial profits of the twenties were not shared with the workers. Since the rise of permanent unions in the post-World War II period profits and wages have not been closely related as there have been no wage cuts despite frequent profit declines in this period.

On the basis of Chart 1, Harvester wages have shown their greatest margins above national manufacturing averages in the periods before 1887 and after 1947. The latter period has probably been the nearest thing to sustained competition in the company's history. Profits after 1953 have been lower than in earlier periods, yet the wage growth rate has been higher than at any peacetime period except the pre-1887 period. How has it been possible to grant high wage increases in this period of low profits and stiff market competition? The explanation cannot be found in the labor market situation since employment at the McCormick Works (and for the entire firm) actually declined during this period, nor in the national labor market scene where 5.5 per cent unemployment indicated a general surplus of labor.

Unionism does give a probable though complex answer to this high rate of wage increase. The frequent strikes of this period – 1947, 1948, 1950, 1952, 1955, 1958 – plus thousands of wildcat stoppages at International Harvester indicate strong union pressure. But the union pressure exerted against the firm is only a part of the answer. In a truly competitive product market situation strikes might have driven the firm to bankruptcy but would have had little success in raising wages. But in the 1947–1960 situation all the firms' major competitors were, for the first time, unionized and subject to the same wage pressures. The union equalized wage costs (or at least wage rates) among all competitors. While the product market competition cut into profits and did cause the firm to resist union wage demands, eventual concessions to the union did not hurt the company's competitive market position. A third aspect of union pressure in this period was the union's successful insistence on wage gains equal to the more profitable auto industry. The fact that the auto industry's rate of wage increases was itself influenced by union pressures implies that the unions at International Harvester may have had to exert more pressure than those in auto to achieve the same rate of increase.

The oligopolistic nature of the product market from 1858 to 1960 with its generally wide profit margins did provide the McCormick Company and International Harvester Company with wide latitude in wage policy. At all times there was leeway to grant wage concessions when faced with union pressure. There was also leeway to pay above market rates for common labor from 1887 to 1896 in order to avoid labor trouble. During certain periods, 1880–1884 for instance, it would appear from the large and growing company earnings that an aggressive union might have received a larger share of the company's income. The answer to the union's shortcoming in this respect is that while the company was financially able to make concessions it was also financially able to refuse them. In destroying the unions in 1886 the company spared no expense — wage concessions to workers while firing union officers, and large capital expenditures to purchase automatic molding machines. In the frequent strike situations since that time the company has shown a willingness to accept long plant shutdowns rather than to make what it thought were undesirable concessions to unions. A firm with a less well protected market position would have had fewer resources with which to resist union pressures. In any period when the union got a foothold, such as 1862–1886 or after 1940, the absence of pure competition in the product market has provided a moderately favorable climate for trade union bargaining pressures.

When there were no unions to pressure the company — 1887–1898, 1905–1913, or 1923–1929 — wage gains were low and the McCormick Works average rate of gain fell below the U.S. manufacturing average. The oligopolistic product market, therefore, appears to have been chiefly permissive, not causal.

Are there any theoretical reasons for doubting these conclusions? Certainly not so far as they apply to the McCormick and International Harvester firms. An individual firm, particularly one with a protected market position, would have no difficulty in making concessions to unions without depriving the firm of necessary capital. Furthermore, if major segments of the industry to which the firm belonged became unionized, as was the situation after 1940, the cost push at all firms could be passed along to the farmer purchasers even though the firms within the industry were competing in the product market. And for short periods, the stockholders could give up what the union gained.

Is there such a thing as a "trust" wage policy? American trusts after 1900 very clearly developed a price policy quite different from the flexible price behavior generally found in competitive industries. Trust price behavior has long specialized in stability during recessions. Sophisticated trusts gradually began not only to resist competitive price cuts but to avoid price gouging when shortages developed. A recent example of this was the price restraint which auto and steel companies showed in the shortages occurring after World War II.

One of the early advocates of stable commodity pricing by trusts was George W. Perkins, J. P. Morgan's right-hand man on the U.S. Steel and International Harvester finance committees. When in 1909 business began to boom following the 1907–1908 recession, U.S. Steel subsidiaries wanted to raise prices. Perkins wrote U.S. Steel President Corey, "Don't let the subsidiaries raise prices. Two or three years ago they raised them too high. We want price stability and are now strong enough to try it in a period of prosperity. The country expects us to make A-No. 1 goods, and to make them at reasonable prices. Our subsidiaries think their function is to get the very last dollar they can when trade conditions make it possible."[3]

From this price policy, born of the trust's need for public goodwill, there stemmed a corollary wage policy. The wage policy, like the price policy, had an eye on public relations. Though anti-union it shunned public and ideological battles with unions. For example, when U.S. Steel was unloading watered stock on the public in 1901, in an effort to avoid the additional adverse publicity of a strike, Perkins and even J. P. Morgan met with union representatives and tried to reach a compromise settlement though the manufacturing officials favored giving the unions no quarter. Because of the strong and growing public suspicion of trusts as expressed in state legislatures, in Congress, and in presidential campaigns, Perkins time and again blocked U.S. Steel wage cuts just as he blocked its price increases.[4]

Independently, at International Harvester Cyrus H. McCormick II was learning the same facts the hard way. In the 1885 strike he blamed himself for alienating the public by having cut wages of common labor. In his 1886 labor union negotiations he first raised the wages of common and semi-skilled labor before locking out the workers. When the 1893 depression struck, he maintained the common labor wage while cutting skilled workmen. In 1904 Cyrus McCormick II did approve hourly wage cuts, but they were in the nature of an increase in weekly hours for the same weekly pay. He felt that this would lessen the chance of a strike. In both 1921 and 1931 the Harvester Company cut wages but it did not lead the parade. In fact in 1931 the first blue collar cut came over two years after the October, 1929, stock crash.

In wage policy the trust sought favorable public relations as well as satisfied employees but prior to the 1940's it never went so far as to accept unionism. Cyrus McCormick II temporarily made union agreements in 1885 and 1903–1904 when he could not open his plants any other way. He destroyed the unions at the first opportunity. George Perkins and Cyrus McCormick II were both strong supporters of the

National Civic League, whose executive secretary, Ralph Easley, worked hard to promote recognition of unionism. Perkins and Judge Elbert Gary of U.S. Steel joined to pay the National Civic League salary of ex-United Mine Worker President John Mitchell. Yet neither they nor Cyrus McCormick II would deal with unions in their own enterprises.

Perkins had approved the Harvester plan in the 1904 recession for breaking with the unions. In the summer of 1907 Perkins masterminded the steel corporation's defeat of the Western Federation of Miners Minnesota ore strike. At great risk to the steel corporation's winter operations, he advised J. P. Morgan, "Better fight it out now while they are small [20,000 men were then on strike] . . . we can't afford to let the Western Miners Association get possession of our mines." [5] Perkins was more willing to fight it out with a radical group like the Western Federation both because he feared it more and because he felt more confident of public sympathy. Upon occasion he was willing to raise wages, i.e., when price increases were contemplated, when profits were good, and labor trouble might call unfavorable attention to the trusts. In 1916 he urged such a policy at U.S. Steel and at Harvester. Perkins' successors in U.S. Steel did not seem to understand this policy or they would have abolished the twelve-hour day before 1923. The Harvester Company did put its steel mill on the three-shift, eight-hour day during World War I and never reverted to the twelve-hour system.

Both Harvester and U.S. Steel maintained stable wages in the 1923–1929 period and attempted to wait out the post-1929 depression without wage cuts. Two years after the crash, along with other big corporations, they were forced to abandon their wage stability program and cut wages.

Harvester history is full of so many exceptions to the above trust wage policy that at Harvester it should be more accurately labeled a "tendency" than a "policy." Except when pushed off its course by unionism, Harvester was more likely than not to purchase labor at market prices. Nevertheless the trust policy of wage stability has been an element in Harvester policy, particularly after the government anti-trust suit was launched in 1912.

8

Summary of Findings

Union Impact

Unionism has been an accompaniment to the periods of more rapid real wage growth. The data of Table 9 record an average real wage growth rate at the McCormick Works of 3.9 per cent for 31 years of unionized peacetime prosperity and only 0.1 per cent for 20 roughly comparable non-union years between 1860 and 1960. Even more significant is the fact that the wage chronologies showing the exact date and nature of wage change and the correspondence of company executives confirm unionism's direct association with most of the firm's major upward wage movements.

Historically, at the McCormick Works the general plant-wide wage increase was clearly of union origin. The first four such wage increases in the history of the company — May, 1867, April, 1885, May, 1886, and May, 1903 — were all strike-born. Making the general increase an annual affair was also clearly of union origin, though this did not occur at the McCormick Works until the end of World War II. This plant- and company-wide, periodic wage increase was fastened on the company by union pressures during the same post-World War II years. It is this pattern of general periodic wage increase which characterizes the high real wage growth rates of recent years.

The detailed wage comparisons amongst three competing agricultural implements firms, McCormick, Deering, and Plano, 1882–1902, lead to two conclusions:

a. The McCormick firm as the only unionized firm paid substantially higher average hourly earnings until its unions were broken in 1886. It shortly thereafter became the lowest wage plant of the three.

b. McCormick unionism in the 1880's had a big wage impact on the non-union neighboring Deering firm. On three occasions when the McCormick workers went on strike during 1885 and 1886 there were quick wage repercussions at the Deering plant. On one occasion the Deering Company raised its wages before the struck McCormick plant had done so. On the third occasion, when the Deering Company lagged several days behind the McCormick raise, the Deering workers went on strike and secured their own raise.

The Plano Company, thirty-five miles from Chicago, escaped the strike wave of 1885–1886 and the wage repercussions from the McCormick plant. By moving its plant to Chicago in 1893 it was able to tap a supply of cheap labor which had been unavailable at Plano. The city-town wage differential at this time, at least for common labor, favored the large city.

Market Demand

In the hundred-year period the state of market demand for labor at the McCormick Works has frequently brought money wage cuts in depressions. It has been singularly weak as a force for raising money wages in peacetime prosperity. In non-union periods of peacetime prosperity, real wages tended to remain relatively stable, 1905–1913, 0.4 per cent per year; to grow very slowly, 1923–1929, 0.9 per cent per year; or even to decline, 1887–1893, −1.2 per cent per year. At the McCormick Works there were no peacetime periods of sustained high real wage growth rates in the absence of unionism.

The inflationary years of 1919–1920, and 1945–1946 are here considered part of the war years because the war caused the inflation. This conclusion does not deny that at the McCormick Works a sufficiently high market demand for labor would be capable of bringing about above average money and even real wage gains in the absence of strong unionism, but merely notes that prior to 1961 the peacetime labor market was not tight enough to have done so. Thus it was that in the peacetime years between 1860–1960 it was the unionized years that stand out as the years of above average money and real wage growth rates.

Correlation, r, of McCormick Works annual percentage money wage change and employment change was .18, significant at the 5 per cent level, for the period 1858–1960. Eliminating war years raised the correlation, r, to .22. Eliminating both wartime and the years when the McCormick Works was unionized raised the correlation, r, to .40, significant at the 5 per cent level.

In the period 1947–1960 McCormick Works wage rates have generally, with the exception of 1949, followed automobile patterns regardless of the state of market demand for labor.

Wage Rigidity

On balance there has been an increase in wage rigidity over the hundred years. The seasonal fluctuations have been eliminated. Prior to 1870 there were regular seasonal changes in wage rates – up in the spring and down in the fall. Depression wage behavior has seen a spectacular long-run increase in rigidity. Prior to the 1930's economic downturns resulted in prompt wage cuts. Strikes by unions as early as 1873 were important in delaying or reversing these cuts and beginning with the post-World War II period have even brought regular wage increases during economic downturns.

On the upswing from economic depressions unionism has throughout the hundred-year period been a substantial force for increasing the upward wage flexibility, reinforcing labor market pressures, and reducing or overcoming the real wage lag which occurs as market forces traditionally raise prices before wages. A calculation of wage movements at the McCormick Works from depression troughs to prosperity peaks in ten peacetime business cycles, 1860–1960, indicates that in six unionized upturns real average hourly earnings rose at an average rate of 5.9 per cent per year, while in four non-unionized upturns real average hourly earnings rose at only 0.7 per cent (Table 19, Chapter 4). Even in the post-World War II inflation, 1946–1948, when annual union agreements regulated the time of the wage increase, the evidence of quit rates and unemployment rates indicates that at International Harvester union pressures pushed wages up farther and faster than would probably have resulted from labor market forces alone. However, since World War II the union-established concept of an increase every year modified by more frequent cost-of-living adjustments has eliminated such sporadic, spectacular strike-fostered increases as 25 per cent in May, 1886, 14 per cent in 1903, 11 per cent in May, 1916.

Productivity

In the short run, real wage growth at the McCormick Works shows little relationship to productivity (Table 24, Chapter 6). A decade-by-decade analysis of the OMH in the farm equipment industry and real wage growth rates at the McCormick Works since 1889 gives a strong inverse relationship (Table 25, Chapter 5).

In the long run (1889 to 1957) McCormick Works and U.S. manufacturing real wage growth rates (both at 2.4 per cent per year) exceeded total factor productivity in the U.S. economy (1.6 per cent) and real net national product per capita (2.0 per cent) (Table 24). But for the pre-1919 period — 1889–1919 — the same measures of productivity exceeded McCormick Works wage growth rates: total factor productivity, 1.4 per cent, real net product per capita, 2.4 per cent, to 1.0 per cent for McCormick Works real AHE growth rate. In the period 1919–1953, McCormick real wage growth rates exceeded total factor productivity and real net product per capita, 1.7 per cent and 1.8 per cent to 3.1 per cent (Table 24). Since McCormick Works wage growth was low in the twenties, the higher rate of wage growth came from the unionized period in the economy since 1933.

Thus, if productivity has provided any limits on wage growth they have been in the short run very loose limits.

The Product Market

The product market, which has varied only from oligopoly to near monopoly and back to oligopoly, has been a major factor in giving the company leeway to meet wage demands and likewise to pay regular dividends to stockholders.

Lack of stiff market competition has almost uniformly brought Harvester profits large enough to permit upward wage flexibility whenever unions demanded it. On the other hand, years of high profits have not generally been reflected in high wages. One of the highest rates of wage growth has been the period 1947–1960. Yet this period has seen the poorest profit showing amongst periods of prosperity in the history of the company (Table 27, Chapter 7). However, even in this period of relatively low profits, union pressures forced the company to match the wage pattern of the vastly more profitable automobile industry. The product market has thus been permissive, not causal, in wage determination.

General Conclusions

To what extent can the conclusions of this study of the McCormick Works be applied to broader groups, manufacturing, railroads, mining, retail and service industries?

It is highly unlikely that the experience of the McCormick Works was unique. The union with which the McCormick Company bargained from 1862 through 1885 was a city-wide union, implying that the wage patterns observed at McCormick were city-wide patterns. The McCormick and Chicago experience was probably typical of industry located in urban centers nationally. On each occasion that unionism reappeared at the McCormick Works — 1903, 1916, 1919, the mid-1930's — it was in the midst of great national surges in union growth. On the other hand, these surges in union growth were frequently slower in reaching the small towns and in some cases bypassed them completely. Consequently, the national wage growth patterns, being averages of union and non-union firms, do not reveal such sharp contrasts between union and non-union periods as at the McCormick Works.

So far as manufacturing is concerned, this study includes data which indicates almost identical wage growth patterns for manufacturing and the McCormick Works after 1900 (Chart 1 and Table 1). But even for the entire period 1860–1960, the movements are, except for 1887–1893, in the same direction. If we divide the prosperous periods from 1860 to 1960 into periods of strong or rapidly growing unionism on the one hand and into periods of weak or slowly growing unionism on the other, we find (Table 9, Chapter 4) that the average growth rate of wages for production workers in manufacturing in the former clearly exceeds that of the latter, 3.3 per cent per year (union) to 1.5 per cent per year (non-union) in money wages, and 3.6 per cent per year (union) to 1.3 per cent per year (non-union) in real wages. This duplicates the findings for the McCormick wage movements. Since the McCormick growth rates were most closely positively correlated with union influence, it is possible that unionism was a cause of the high growth rate periods in national manufacturing. While it is true that to some extent unionism is positively correlated with prosperity, there are wide differences in the degree of unionism in different periods of prosperity. The periods 1923–1929 and 1908–1913 demonstrate that it was possible to have prosperity without strong or growing unionism. Since this study is based on rates of wage growth in roughly comparable periods of peacetime prosperity, but with differing degrees of unionism, the impact of this slight cor-relation between unionism and prosperity has been eliminated.

In the period from 1860 to 1900 the rates of wage growth between the McCormick Works and U.S. manufacturing diverge somewhat, being higher at McCormick prior to 1887, during which period the McCormick Works had strong unions. When unionism at McCormick was destroyed in 1886 its wage growth rate fell below that in manufac-turing. Clearly, many segments of manufacturing departed enough from pure competition in the product market so that union influence would have been able to bring higher wage rates just as at the McCor-mick Works. On the other hand, wage growth rates in some of the more competitive sections of manufacturing, such as textiles following the growth of the industry in the South, probably would not respond so readily to expansion of union membership. These hypotheses on the causes of wage movement in manufacturing should, of course, be checked by several case studies of payroll books similar to the study of the McCormick Works.

Wages in manufacturing as in the McCormick Works show peacetime market demand to be an important factor in lowering wage growth rates in depressions, but weak as a force for raising wages in prosperity unless accompanied by strong unions. Nor does the restriction of immi-gration after World War I appear to have created labor shortages.

Table 16 of Chapter 5 indicates that in the non-union prosperity of 1923–1929 wage gains both real and in money terms were lower than in the 1909–1913 prosperous period of high immigration. The generally high wage growth rates in manufacturing of the 1933–1960 period were certainly not due to labor shortages as revealed by the figures in (3), Table 16.

For manufacturing as for the McCormick Works the wage recovery from ten depression troughs to the succeeding prosperity peaks brings decreased wage rigidity (Table 19, Chapter 5) in the presence of stronger unionism and, of course, Chart 1 indicates increased wage rigidity on the downward swing of the cycles of 1938, 1949, 1954, and 1958, after unionism had become firmly established.

There is no evidence (Table 24, Chapter 6) to support the view that the high wage growth rates in U.S. manufacturing in recent years (since 1933) are due to higher productivity.

This study provides no wage growth rate data for other industries, but if we project the findings of the McCormick study we would expect to find wage rate growth high in the pre-1900 period, reflecting the early union growth in such industries as railroads and construction. In the 1920's when unionism in these industries was substantially stronger than in manufacturing, they did have higher growth rates.[1]

In the coal mining industry the wage trends closely parallel the strength of the United Mine Workers Union. Due to the competitive nature of the product market and the failure of the union to organize the South, wages fell precipitously during the 1920's. During this period union membership declined steadily as the industry expanded in the non-union South.

In the restaurant and service industries there exists very little historical wage information, but the current wage advantage enjoyed by a highly unionized sector such as the retail food supermarkets is supportative of the conclusions of the McCormick Works study.[2]

The large amount of unionism today with its heavy spillover effects makes it difficult to isolate the wage effect of unionism. The McCormick study, by permitting observation of varying amounts of unionism over time, aids in isolating this factor. Not only does this study imply that unionism is an important wage determining factor today, but that even in the last century when unionism was relatively weaker than today it was a significant factor in wage determination.

To repeat here one of the conclusions of Chapter 4: the emphasis given in this study to the influence of unionism as a causal factor in wage increases in no sense denies the important role of labor market forces in wage determination. But it is a finding of this study that the substantial variation in wage growth rates which has occurred in the various periods of peacetime prosperity between 1860 and 1960 are not accounted for by variations in labor market conditions.

Reference Material

Appendix A

AHE, McCormick Works and U.S. Manufacturing

This table contains the basic year-by-year comparative wage data for the McCormick Works and U.S. manufacturing. The series for U.S. manufacturing is based on data from Clarence D. Long, "The Illusion of Wage Rigidity," *Review of Economics and Statistics*, 42, No. 2, Part 1 (May, 1960): 150–51; these data also include estimates of fringe benefits from (for 1939–1957) Albert Rees, *New Measures of Wage-Earner Compensation in Manufacturing, 1914–1957*, Occasional Paper No. 75 (Princeton, N.J.: National Bureau of Economic Research, 1960), Table 1, pp. 3–4, and (for 1958–1960) from Economic Councils, *Annual Report to the President* (Washington, D.C.: GPO, 1962), Table 22, p. 177. These data also include overtime wages; while this brings some distortion during World War II in comparison with the data for the McCormick Works, the distortion from 1947 to 1960 is minor because overtime did not cumulatively enlarge during this period.

The data for computing McCormick Works' money wage comes (for 1849, 1858–1914) from McCormick Works Payroll books in the McCormick Collection, and (for 1915–1960) from I.H.Co. records in Chicago. For the years 1849, and 1858–1914, the figures are AHE of a typical payroll period during the peak production season — the first payroll period in April — except for 1867 and 1877 when a strike and a flood respectively led to use of data from adjacent pay periods. For the years 1915–1924, company-compiled data based on annual averages were used. For the years 1925–1960, company-compiled data for the month of April were used.

For the years 1849, 1859–1940, McCormick AHE includes overtime. However, the actual payment of overtime was very limited except for the years 1918–1920. During this period acceptance of war orders forced the I.H.Co. to move to the eight-hour day with time-and-one-half pay for work over eight hours per day, while it continued to work nine hours per day. In 1921 overtime after eight hours was discontinued. Thus the use of straight-time AHE

133

beginning in 1941 merely continues what was an essentially straight-time series due to the company's sparing use of overtime prior to World War II.

The data for McCormick Works' real wages are also based on the company records cited above, but have been adjusted by the cost-of-living index from Long, "The Illusion of Wage Rigidity," pp. 150–51.

Fringe benefits have been added to the McCormick wage data from the sources cited above on the assumption that I.H.Co.'s fringe benefits were the same percentage of wages as for all U.S. manufacturing. It is also assumed that before 1939 all fringe benefits were so small as to be negligible.

Year	McCormick money wage (1)	McCormick real wage (2)	U.S. manufacturing money wage (3)
1849	.113	.386	—
1858	.097	.311	.097
1859	.093	.295	.093
1860	.095	.286	.095
1861	.098	.293	.097
1862	.099	.261	.106
1863	.135	.291	.107
1864	.170	.290	.122
1865	.204	.349	.134
1866	.200	.368	.138
1867	.228	.404	.141
1868	.221	.452	.142
1869	.225	.475	.144
1870	.235	.530	.145
1871	.233	.541	.147
1872	.226	.511	.148
1873	.261	.608	.150
1874	.238	.563	.144
1875	.206	.510	.140
1876	.178	.504	.137
1877	.185	.467	.132
1878	.172	.467	.128
1879	.162	.449	.126
1880	.187	.512	.130
1881	.216	.590	.135
1882	.224	.614	.138
1883	.212	.592	.142
1884	.215	.611	.144
1885	.180	.526	.141
1886	.201	.600	.143

Year	McCormick money wage (1)	McCormick real wage (2)	U.S. manufacturing money wage (3)
1887	.216	.639	.149
1888	.208	.615	.150
1889	.213	.649	.151
1890	.213	.655	.153
1891	.192	.585	.153
1892	.203	.623	.154
1893	.188	.586	.160
1894	.182	.593	.147
1895	.172	.573	.146
1896	.182	.607	.146
1897	.175	.591	.147
1898	.183	.618	.144
1899	.194	.655	.152
1900	.187	.623	.158
1901	.189	.624	.165
1902	.194	.632	.172
1903	.209	.666	.178
1904	.220	.692	.176
1905	.218	.686	.179
1906	.222	.692	.193
1907	.218	.649	.200
1908	.220	.671	.192
1909	.216	.665	.193
1910	.228	.673	.204
1911	.238	.702	.208
1912	.229	.662	.211
1913	.254	.722	.223
1914	.262	.734	.223
1915	.268	.742	.230
1916	.291	.750	.267
1917	.375	.822	.314
1918	.477	.890	.397
1919	.555	.899	.477
1920	.675	.945	.582
1921	.665	1.046	.527
1922	.522	.876	.491
1923	.585	.964	.522
1924	.611	1.003	.547
1925	.615	.990	.547
1926	.604	.960	.548

Year	McCormick money wage (1)	McCormick real wage (2)	U.S. manufacturing money wage (3)
1927	.608	.973	.550
1928	.632	1.041	.562
1929	.626	1.031	.566
1930	.633	1.057	.552
1931	.642	1.193	.515
1932	.595	1.226	.446
1933	.571	1.263	.442
1934	.613	1.293	.532
1935	.646	1.246	.550
1936	.696	1.429	.556
1937	.826	1.632	.624
1938	.826	1.645	.627
1939	.839	1.702	.638
1940	.844	1.698	.670
1941	.935	1.841	.737
1942	.980	1.710	.864
1943	1.058	1.715	.975
1944	1.147	1.850	1.05
1945	1.184	1.873	1.06
1946	1.252	1.920	1.13
1947	1.424	1.833	1.30
1948	1.583	1.880	1.41
1949	1.708	2.024	1.46
1950	1.745	2.082	1.55
1951	2.021	2.208	1.73
1952	2.223	2.367	1.83
1953	2.228	2.355	1.94
1954	2.251	2.362	1.97
1955	2.293	2.414	2.05
1956	2.418	2.529	2.15
1957	2.589	2.607	2.27
1958	2.795	2.721	2.36
1959	3.003	2.913	2.46
1960	3.130	2.981	2.56

Appendix B

Wage and Employment Changes at the McCormick Works, 1858–1960;
National Unemployment Rates, 1900–1960

Year	Annual per cent change in AHE, McCormick Works (1)	Annual per cent employment change at McCormick Works (2)	Unemployment as a per cent of non-farm employees[a] (3)
1859	−4.1	—[b]	
1860	2.2	2.9	
1861	3.2	−13.1	
1862	1.0	1.8	
1863	36.4	−10.8	
1864	25.9	99.5	
1865	20.0	−26.7	
1866	−2.0	62.6	
1867	14.0	−19.2	
1868	−4.3	−3.7	
1869	1.8	18.8	
1870	4.4	10.3	
1871	−0.9	−7.1	
1872	−3.22	—[c]	
1873	15.7	46.4	
1874	−8.8	−26.5	
1875	−13.5	11.4	
1876	−4.1	−1.3	
1877	−6.6	−23.2	
1878	−6.8	57.7	
1879	−5.8	−1.3	

137

Year	Annual per cent change in AHE, McCormick Works (1)	Annual per cent employment change at McCormick Works (2)	Unemployment as a per cent of non-farm employees [a] (3)
1880	15.4	1.7	
1881	15.2	38.8	
1882	3.9	35.3	
1883	−5.4	−8.4	
1884	1.4	0.3	
1885	−16.3	10.7	
1886	11.7	−11.0	
1887	7.5	26.1	
1888	−3.7	2.0	
1889	2.4	−9.4	
1890	0.	1.4	
1891	−9.9	−20.5	
1892	5.5	34.0	
1893	−7.2	16.7	
1894	−3.2	−17.3	
1895	−5.5	−5.4	
1896	5.8	26.7	
1897	−3.9	4.5	
1898	4.6	15.7	
1899	6.0	26.3	
1900	−3.6	60.2	8.7
1901	1.1	1.1	4.3
1902	2.6	54.8	4.5
1903	7.7	−15.0	4.4
1904	5.3	−17.2	7.9
1905	−0.9	13.7	5.1
1906	1.8	15.4	1.4
1907	−1.8	15.3	2.9
1908	0.9	−21.6	13.5
1909	−1.8	−1.0	8.2
1910	5.6	36.0	9.1
1911	4.4	4.6	9.5
1912	−3.8	−11.08	7.9
1913	10.9	24.8	6.4
1914	3.1	−23.8	11.9
1915	2.3	−11.8	14.3
1916	8.6	−5.1	7.1
1917	28.9	16.3	7.0
1918	27.2	−5.5	2.1

Year	Annual per cent change in AHE, McCormick Works (1)	Annual per cent employment change at McCormick Works (2)	Unemployment as a per cent of non-farm employees[a] (3)
1919	16.4	−5.2	3.4
1920	21.6	13.2	5.8
1921	−1.5	−28.7	16.9
1922	−21.5	−36.4	10.9
1923	12.1	32.3	4.6
1924	4.4	11.2	8.0
1925	0.7	−14.4	5.9
1926	−1.8	59.5	2.8
1927	0.7	−3.4	5.9
1928	3.9	7.2	6.4
1929	−0.9	4.1	4.7
1930	1.1	−5.3	13.0
1931	1.4	−37.6	23.3
1932	−7.3	−24.5	34.0
1933	−4.0	12.1	35.3
1934	7.4	45.4	30.6
1935	5.4	37.7	28.4
1936	7.7	39.5	23.9
1937	18.7	−22.9	20.0
1938	0.0	1.6	26.4
1939	1.6	−25.9	23.8
1940	0.6	4.7	20.2
1941	10.8	23.5	13.3
1942	4.8	−20.4	6.3
1943	8.0	12.4	2.5
1944	8.4	30.0	1.6
1945	3.2	−21.0	2.5
1946	5.7	0.0[d]	5.2
1947	13.7	9.1[e]	4.7
1948	11.2	10.8	4.5
1949	7.9	−7.5	7.3
1950	2.2	3.4	6.6
1951	16.2	3.2	3.8
1952	9.7	6.7	3.4
1953	0.2	−2.4	3.2
1954	1.0	−17.0	6.3
1955	1.8	7.0	5.0
1956	5.5	−2.1	4.7
1957	7.1	−7.0	5.3

Year	Annual per cent change in AHE, McCormick Works (1)	Annual per cent employment change at McCormick Works (2)	Unemployment as a per cent of non-farm employees [a] (3)
1958	8.0	−8.2	8.4
1959	7.4	16.9	6.4
1960	4.2	−7.7	6.4

[a] Data unavailable until 1900.

[b] Data unavailable.

[c] October, 1871, was the time of the Chicago fire, and employment for 1872 was greatly reduced. The per cent changes in employment are calculated for April, 1871 to April, 1873.

[d] April, 1946, comes in the midst of a long strike and employment is abnormally low, so 1946 is assumed to have the same employment as 1945.

[e] In the period 1947–1960, since the McCormick Works was an obsolete plant, employment changes in the firm have been substituted.

Sources: (1), basic data from Appendix A.

(2), basic data from McCormick Works payroll books, 1859–1914 in the McCormick Collection, 1915–1960 from I.H.Co. files, Chicago.

(3), unemployment, 1900–1958, Wm. G. Bowen, *Wage Behavior in the Post-War Period* (Princeton, N.J.: Princeton University Press, 1960), pp. 100–101; 1959–1960 from the *Economic Report of the President*, 1963, Table C–19, p. 194, and C–25, p. 201.

Appendix C

Extent of Work Stoppages, 1881–1960, United States

| Period | Work Stoppages Beginning in Period | | |
| | Number | Workers Involved | |
		Number (thousands)	Per cent of total employed
1881	477	130	— a
1882	476	159	— a
1883	506	170	— a
1884	485	165	— a
1885	695	258	— a
1886	1,572	610	— a
1887	1,503	439	— a
1888	946	163	— a
1889	1,111	260	— a
1890	1,897	373	4.2
1891	1,786	330	3.6
1892	1,359	239	2.5
1893	1,375	288	3.2
1894	1,404	690	8.3
1895	1,255	407	4.4
1896	1,066	249	2.8
1897	1,110	416	4.3
1898	1,098	263	2.6
1899	1,838	432	3.9
1900	1,839	568	4.9
1901	3,012	564	4.6

Period	Work Stoppages Beginning in Period		
	Number	Workers Involved	
		Number (thousands)	Per cent of total employed
1902	3,240	692	5.4
1903	3,648	788	5.9
1904	2,419	574	4.3
1905	2,186	302	2.1
1906–1913	— a	— a	— a
1914	1,204	— a	— a
1915	1,593	— a	— a
1916	3,789	1,600	8.4
1917	4,450	1,230	6.3
1918	3,353	1,240	6.2
1919	3,630	4,160	20.8
1920	3,411	1,460	7.2
1921	2,385	1,100	6.4
1922	1,112	1,610	8.7
1923	1,553	757	3.5
1924	1,249	655	3.1
1925	1,301	428	2.0
1926	1,035	330	1.5
1927	707	330	1.4
1928	604	314	1.3
1929	921	289	1.2
1930	637	183	.8
1931	810	342	1.6
1932	841	324	1.8
1933	1,695	1,170	6.3
1934	1,856	1,470	7.2
1935	2,014	1,120	5.2
1936	2,172	789	3.1
1937	4,740	1,860	7.2
1938	2,772	688	2.8
1939	2,613	1,170	4.7
1940	2,508	577	2.3
1941	4,288	2,360	8.4
1942	2,968	840	2.8
1943	3,752	1,980	6.9
1944	4,956	2,120	7.0
1945	4,750	3,470	12.2
1946	4,985	4,600	16.5

Period	Work Stoppages Beginning in Period		
	Number	Workers Involved	
		Number (thousands)	Per cent of total employed
1947	3,693	2,170	6.5
1948	3,419	1,960	5.5
1949	3,606	3,030	9.0
1950	4,843	2,410	6.9
1951	4,737	2,220	5.5
1952	5,117	3,540	8.8
1953	5,091	2,400	5.6
1954	3,468	1,530	3.7
1955	4,320	2,650	6.2
1956	3,825	1,900	4.3
1957	3,673	1,390	3.1
1958	3,694	2,060	4.8
1959	3,708	1,880	4.3
1960	3,333	1,320	3.0

[a] Data unavailable.

Source: United States Department of Labor, Bureau of Labor Statistics, *Handbook of Labor Statistics* (Washington, D.C.: GPO, 1950), p. 142, Table E–2.

Appendix D

A Century of Occupational Differentials in Manufacturing [1]

The interest in occupational differentials has blossomed profusely since the famous study by Harry Ober in 1948. By now, the resultant body of theory has somewhat over-extended itself in relation to the supporting facts. Two painfully obvious gaps in occupational wage data are: a lack of data on occupational differentials prior to 1907; and an absence, since 1907, of continuous year-to-year data on manufacturing. The Ober study is limited to spot surveys at ten- or twelve-year intervals.[2] The resultant extrapolation as to occupational differential movements gives one little confidence in the current body of theory. This study in a limited way fills in some of the missing gaps of factual information. Based primarily on payroll records of one company, it gives a continuous picture of occupational differentials from 1858 through 1959.

The data for Chart D-1 are based on original payroll ledgers of production workers in the McCormick Works. In calculating the McCormick Works' occupational differential ratio on Chart D-1, it was necessary, because of data limitations, to use at different times two different concepts of skilled labor. From 1858 to 1897 the skilled worker concept used was the straight-time mean hourly rate of the upper sextile of day-rate production employees after removal of supervisors. From 1888 to 1959 (ten years of overlap with the sextile concept) the skilled worker concept used was that of the straight-time mean hourly rate of pattern shop craftsmen. Spot checks show that the pattern shop wage trends were similar to those of other skilled crafts from 1888 to 1941. In this year (1941) the pattern shop established a separate bargaining unit under the Patternmakers League of North America. From 1941 wage trends of skilled craftsmen diverge somewhat, depending on the nature of the collective bargaining arrangement for each craft.

The Underdeveloped Country Hypothesis

Much of current occupational differential theory is devoted to explaining an assumed long-run decline in occupational differentials. Presumably, when a country is in the early stages of industrialization, common labor is plentiful and skilled labor rare. Industrialization and education gradually make skilled labor plentiful and reduce the premium which skilled labor receives in the early stages of industrialization.[3] The Ober-Kaninen data on manufacturing differentials (Table D-1), showing an almost steady decline since 1907, are one of the mainstays of this thesis as it applies to the United States.

The McCormick data of Chart D-1 raise doubts about the underdeveloped country hypothesis at least insofar as it assumes that high 1907 differentials were due to the immature state of the United States economy. From the vantage of the 100-year McCormick record (Chart D-1) the wide differential of 1907 appears not as evidence of higher differentials in our less industrialized past, but merely one of a half dozen similar peaks in a recurring rise and fall of differentials.

If we look further at the lack of trend in differentials in early wage surveys of the 1860–1890 period as listed in Table D-1, we may have serious doubts that America since 1860 has experienced the wide differentials attributed to underdeveloped countries.

There are several possible reasons why America might have escaped the high wage differentials often found in the early stages of industrialization. By contrast with currently underdeveloped countries, American industrialization proceeded at a slower pace. Except for a few skilled weavers enticed from England in the 1820's, early American industry may have had time to train many of its own skilled workers. Secondly, from 1830 to 1873 America's cheap and abundant land resources provided alternative opportunities for common labor which kept its rates abnormally high. America in the early stages of industrialization never possessed the surplus of common labor which existed in Europe and in currently underdeveloped countries. Thirdly, during the early stages of industrialization, 1840–1890, immigration came from the more advanced industrialized countries of northern Europe. This may actually have supplied a surplus of skilled workers from 1850 onward.

The Cessation of Immigration

A second explanation[4] for the supposed long-run narrowing of differentials since 1907 as revealed in the Ober study is that cessation of immigration during and since World War I has brought about a relative shortage of common labor. This argument has this much to be said for it. Certainly, the relative position of common labor would be no better had a net of one million unskilled immigrants been added annually since 1916. But cessation of immigration has not been followed in fact by a growing shortage of unskilled labor. The changing technology in which machines replace labor

Chart D-1. Occupational Differentials at the McCormick Works, 1858–1959

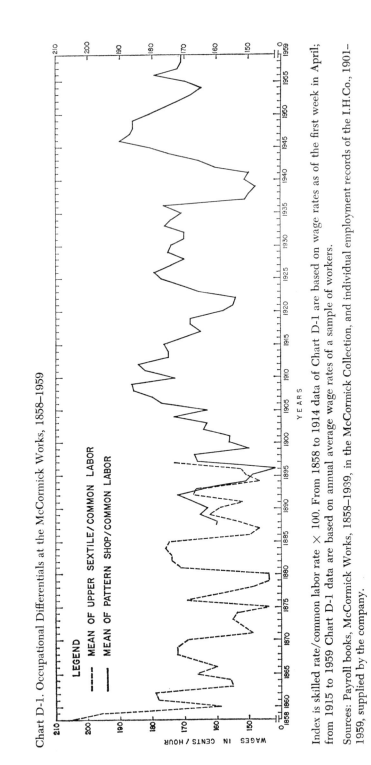

Index is skilled rate/common labor rate × 100. From 1858 to 1914 data of Chart D-1 are based on wage rates as of the first week in April; from 1915 to 1959 Chart D-1 data are based on annual average wage rates of a sample of workers.

Sources: Payroll books, McCormick Works, 1858–1939, in the McCormick Collection, and individual employment records of the I.H.Co., 1901–1959, supplied by the company.

has so reduced the demand for common labor and the stepped-up rural-urban migration has so increased the quantity, that common labor has been in surplus supply even in our prosperous periods.

The widening differential at the McCormick Works from 1921 through 1926 (see Chart D-1) demonstrates that the cessation of immigration did not result in a shortage of unskilled labor in this labor market. The compression of differentials which occurred in 1936–1937 (Chart D-1) cannot be attributed to a shortage of common labor but was due to unionization by an

TABLE D-1

Ober-Kaninen Data: Skilled/Common Labor Ratio

1907	207
1915–1919	175
1931–1932	180
1937–1940	165
1945–1947	155
1952–1953	137

Sources: 1907–1947, Harry Ober, "Occupational Wage Differentials, 1907–1947," *Monthly Labor Review*, 67 (August 1948).

1952–1953, Toivo P. Kaninen, "Occupational Wage Relationships in Manufacturing, 1952–1953," ibid., 76 (Nov., 1953): 1171.

industrial union. It took place in the midst of a substantial common labor surplus. During World War II all labor was scarce. War Labor Board policy, by permitting special wage increases for skilled craftsmen, implied that skilled labor shortages were the more severe. Since World War II, rapid technological change has provided a growing surplus of common labor.

Effects of Immigration

Early immigration from 1848 to 1900 presumably included many skilled workers from the more advanced industrial countries of northern Europe. This immigration may have helped prevent the substantial premiums for skilled workers which are normal in the early stages of industrialization. At the McCormick Works immigration from Sweden was a source of skilled woodworkers during the 1870's. During the 1890's an apparent surplus of patternmakers caused their rates to fall gradually during most of the decade.

After 1900 the change in immigration from the northern European industrial countries to the eastern and southern European agricultural countries may have brought a relative surplus of unskilled labor. At almost the same time (1898–1904) skilled workers were engulfed in a nation-wide tide of unionism. McCormick pattern shop rates rose an average of 23 per cent between 1900 and 1908, while common labor rates stood almost still. Nationally, these same trends, heavy immigration from agricultural countries and a wave of skilled trade unionism, may well have caused the 1907 occupational differential high found by Ober.

Occupational Differentials in Three Wartime Inflations

Economists have considered it almost axiomatic that wartime brings compression of differentials, but it has never been clear why this should be so. Presumably, inflation has something to do with it, but why should inflation and a tight labor market affect common labor more favorably than skilled labor?

TABLE D-2

Occupational Differentials in Manufacturing Based on Data From Three Government Wage Surveys

(Indices are skilled labor/common labor × 100)

Year	Western cities[a] (1)	Eastern cities (2)	Aldrich report[b] (3)	Weeks report (4)
1860	—[c]	—[c]	169	157
1865	—[c]	—[c]	168	169
1870	161	154	176	172
1875	160	157	179	172
1880	174	181	173	171
1885	172	161	170	—[c]
1890	169	168	170	—[c]

[a] U.S. Department of Labor.
[b] Nelson W. Aldrich, *Wholesale Prices, Wages and Transportation* (52 Cong., 2 sess., Senate Report 1394, pt. 2, Washington, March 3, 1893).
[c] Data unavailable.

Sources: (1), (2), Ratios are composed of wage rates of five skilled occupations divided by common labor average rates; the five occupations selected from *Bulletin of the Department of Labor, No. 18,* Carroll D. Wright, ed. (Washington, D.C.: GPO, 1898), are blacksmiths, boilermakers, iron molders, machinists, and patternmakers. Clarence D. Long, *Wages and Earnings in the United States 1860–1960* (Princeton, N.J.: Princeton University Press, 1960), pp. 137–40. Aldrich, *Wholesale Prices.*

(3), Ratios are composed of average of wage rates of five skilled occupations divided by common labor average rate; from Aldrich Report data as compiled by Long, ibid., p. 154. Joseph D. Weeks, "Report on the Statistics of Wages in the Manufacturing Industries with Supplementary Reports on the Average Retail Prices of Necessaries of Life and on Trade Societies, and Strikes and Lockouts," in U.S. Bureau of the Census, *Report of the Census of 1880* (Washington, D.C.: GPO, 1881), pp. ix–xi.

(4), Ratios are composed of average of wages of five skilled occupations divided by common labor average; from Weeks Report data as compiled by Long in *Wages and Earnings,* pp. 137–40. *Bulletin No. 18,* pp. 665–82.

APPENDIX D 149

To get more perspective on the effect of wartime inflation on wage differentials Chart D-2 has been prepared. For Chart D-2 wage differentials have been calculated several times a year for each of the three wars. Thus, we see the effect on differentials of each major wage change.

The Civil War and World War I had in common an early decline in differentials. The causes, however, seem to differ in each case. The Civil War differential declined precipitously from April to September, 1862. This was due to three successive wage increases, each a flat 12.5 cents per day given to common and skilled labor alike. In some cases skilled labor was even bypassed. Turnover of common labor during this period was high. Apparently, alternative opportunities of the burgeoning business boom and of army enlistment held a special attraction to common labor. The big increase, 33 per cent, in common labor rates, which occurred between April and September, 1862, was well above the cost of living.

Market forces somehow were slower in reaching skilled labor. The skilled molders, therefore, took things into their own hands, conducting several strikes during 1863 and 1864.[5] Skilled workers were now given double increments and soon regained much of the lost differential. Toward the end of the war increased turnover of skilled workers aided them in holding their own, even though they failed to regain the pre-war differential.

The World War I period covered in Chart D-2 is not exactly comparable with the other two war periods, since America did not enter a shooting war until 1917, yet Chart D-2 covers the whole period 1916–1919. In the World War I period differentials fell more (176 to 149) than in the Civil War (178 to 166).

As in the Civil War, differentials fell in the early part of the war. The cause, however, appears to be quite different. In 1916 the Harvester Company began cutting piece rates and reducing the work week due to a temporary lull in business. The result was a strike started by the girls in the twine mill. It spread to the foundry and then to the entire plant and lasted for about one month.[6] The settlement brought a 25 per cent hourly increase for common labor and 16 per cent for the pattern shop. Subsequent increases in 1916 and early 1917 likewise favored common labor. While strikes by unskilled labor began the process of narrowing the World War I differentials, higher turnover of common labor continued it.

The company made efforts to widen differentials, favoring patternmakers, in the spring increases of 1918 and 1919. A new strike[7] by unskilled labor in 1919 cut differentials again. Pattern shop turnover was extremely low even at the height of production in 1918, yet war production must have brought about tremendous shortages of skilled workmen. It would appear that labor market forces have less effect on industrial skilled labor in wartime than might be expected. This is because skilled labor has some reluctance about giving up its preferred position for an obviously temporary advantage in higher paying war industries. Common labor has no such inhibitions.

Skilled labor at the McCormick Works in World War I did not unionize

Chart D-2. Occupational Differentials in Three Wars

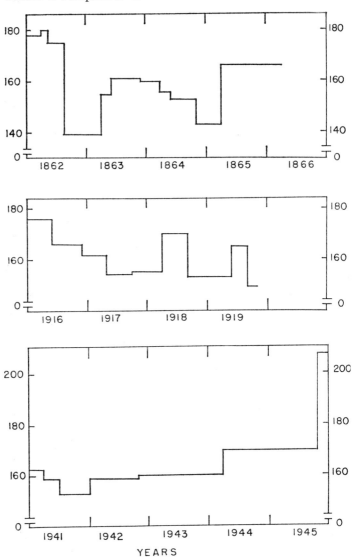

Top: The Civil War. Index is mean of upper sextile/common labor × 100.

Middle: World War I. Index is mean of pattern shop/common labor × 100.

Bottom: World War II. Index is mean of pattern shop/common labor × 100.

nor move to more attractive jobs. It was, therefore, less successful in preserving its wage differentials than its predecessors during the Civil War. Two of the large cuts in differentials occurred as settlements to the strikes of 1916 and 1919. In both these strikes unskilled labor took the leadership.

In World War II, instead of the compression of the two previous wars, we find significant widening of differentials (see Chart D-2.) This appears to conflict with the trend of the Ober-Kaninen data with its broad coverage of manufacturing which does show moderate narrowing from 165 for 1937–1940 to 155 for 1945–1947. The Ober-Kaninen data, however, because of spotty timing, has missed the widening of differentials which apparently occurred in several metalworking industries during the actual conduct of hostilities. If we look at the wage chronologies[8] of auto and steel we find that they conform to the Harvester pattern of widening differentials during World War II. Actually, any narrowing of differentials in auto occurred before and after, not during, the war.

These growing differentials in manufacturing were the result of War Labor Board concessions to skilled workmen. They were permitted under a variety of rationales, not always frankly revealed by the language of the Board decisions.

Five Periods of Non-Inflationary Prosperity

Current theory on the effects of cyclical changes is summarized by Kerr: "The standard statement is that the differentials narrow in prosperity. . . ."[9]

The 100-year McCormick Works' record gives little support to Kerr's generalization, at least in periods of peacetime prosperity. In three of these five prosperous periods (Chart D-1) — 1879–1882, 1900–1907, 1921–1929 — there was a spectacular widening of differentials. In one period, 1870–1873, the differential narrowed. In the 1949–1957 period there is no consistent trend.

Before looking at possible external labor market causes of the widening during prosperity it is interesting to note that in three of the cases of widening — 1879–1882, 1900–1907, and 1921–1929 — a part of the cause may be merely the fact that the preceding periods witnessed severe compression. Thus, internal skilled worker dissatisfaction with the preceding narrowing (Chart D-1) — 1873–1879, 1893–1899, and 1916–1921 — may have exerted pressure on management for restoring customary differentials with returning prosperity.

On the labor market side is the likelihood that the recessions which preceded these prosperous periods developed an accumulation of unskilled labor which for several years acted as a depressant on common labor rates. Furthermore, such recessions must have curtailed new apprenticeships and otherwise interrupted normal training of new skilled workers. Thus, periods of prosperity which follow closely upon periods of unemployment might logically be expected to have a surplus of common labor and a shortage of skilled labor.

In the only prosperous period (1870–1873) in which differentials narrowed, the narrowing occurred in one year, 1871, when common labor rates rose from 15 cents per hour to 17.5 cents per hour, probably due to a shortage of common labor. The 1949–1957 period of prosperity has occurred in a managed era. Unions and management are both conscious of differentials and deliberately prevent the wide fluctuations of the past.

Occupation Differentials in Six Recessions

Recessions, like prosperity, at the McCormick Works affected differentials quite differently from the predicted behavior. Reynolds and Taft describe the expected movements as follows: "It seems reasonable to expect that wage differentials will widen during a period of serious unemployment. Workers dislodged from higher occupations swell the supply of common labor, and new entrants to the labor force are restricted to low-skilled work." [10]

Recessions at McCormick's compressed differentials in 1858, 1873–1879, and 1893–1894. In 1884, 1920–1921, and 1929–1933, wage cuts were strictly proportional and thus had no effect on differentials. The 100-year record gives no support to the view that recessions widen differentials.

The compression of differentials in 1858 was slight. The large compression occurring from 1859 to 1860 (Chart D-1) cannot be considered as part of the recession of 1858, since it was due to the rise in common labor rate from 62 to 75 cents per day.

In the long depression of 1873–1879 there were five successive wage cuts, on balance substantially narrowing differentials. Compression occurred because common labor was exempted from the last three, probably to avoid provoking hard-pressed workers into desperate action.

The company's equal percentage wage cut for all workers, including common labor, in the brief recession of 1884 resulted in violent strike action at the McCormick Works and the company was forced to rescind it. The memory of this was so strong that in the recession beginning in 1893 all cuts of the first three years completely exempted common labor, despite skilled labor cuts in 1893 and 1894. Thus, the depression of the nineties stood out as a period of narrowing differentials primarily due to management's reluctance to cut common labor.

In the recession of 1921 the wage cuts were proportional. The first cut was exactly 20 per cent for all workers; the second was 12.5 per cent. Why was management bold enough to cut common labor proportionately in 1921? The reason is that common labor had fared relatively well in the wartime inflation so that by 1920 differentials were already narrow and even common labor was considered to be above the subsistence level. Likewise, in the recession of 1929–1933 Harvester wage cuts were strictly proportional and no change in differentials occurred.

There is absolutely no evidence at the McCormick Works to support a theory of widening differentials in depressions. The reluctance of management to push common labor to desperation has frequently resulted in less than proportional cuts for common labor.

Influence of Unionism on Occupational Differentials

There is no consensus among wage theorists on the influence of unionism on occupational differentials.

The first union observed at the McCormick Works was the Iron Molders' Union, Local 23. It was a union of skilled craftsmen, arising in late 1862 after a severe wage compression had already taken place. Local 23 conducted six strikes during the Civil War and was certainly a major force in reversing the narrowing trend which dominated the first year of the Civil War (Chart D-2).

In 1867 the first plant-wide strike occurred and the settlement was the first proportional increase, 10 per cent for all. In 1886 a three-union bargaining committee, including an industrially oriented Knights of Labor assembly, gained big increases for common labor and for helpers, substantially narrowing differentials for a decade.

From 1900 to 1904 there was a nationwide surge toward unionism. All groups of workers participated, but it was sparked by skilled workers. The Machinists struck the McCormick Works in 1900 and with other skilled trades continued as a widening force until at least 1904. The interest of skilled workers in unionism no doubt played a part in raising pattern shop rates 23 per cent from 1900 to 1908 while common labor rose only 6 per cent. Heavy immigration, no doubt, retarded common labor rates from 1900 through 1908.

At the McCormick Works high or low differentials have always set in motion countervailing forces. The slowness of the rise in common labor wages brought restlessness which began narrowing the differential during 1912. By World War I it was the unskilled who led the strikes of 1916 and 1919 and helped narrow the differentials of this period.

Union influence is next seen in the mid-thirties when the McCormick plant workers joined the industrially structured Farm Equipment Workers, CIO. In this union the egalitarian sentiment was exceptionally strong. General increases of equal absolute amounts appeared for the first time in the history of the company. Differentials tumbled rapidly.

The pattern shop workers shortly thereafter (1941) joined a separate union and from 1941 to 1946 succeeded in pushing the pattern shop/common labor rate to its highest point in history (Chart D-1; Chart D-2). Moreover, during this period the Pattern Makers League abolished long-standing differentials among patternmakers. In 1941 there existed 7 sub-classifications of patternmakers and differentials among patternmakers were as high as 137. By 1946 all pattern shop craftsmen carried the label "patternmaker" and received the same rate.

To note the difference in differential movements which is due to the structure of union bargaining, it is interesting to compare differentials of two groups of skilled workers in the McCormick Works, one (patternmakers) which broke away from the industrial union unit in 1941 and the other (millwrights) which remained in the industrial bargaining unit. The millwright-common labor differential widened during the war as did that of the patternmaker-common labor, but in the immediate post-war period the millwrights lost their wartime gains whereas the patternmakers extended theirs.

Thus, unionism at the McCormick Works has narrowed, widened, or preserved existing differentials, depending on the groups of workers controlling the union. With all production workers unionized, differentials are getting close scrutiny. The amplitude of their fluctuations will decline. The recent evolution of labor agreements at International Harvester bears this out. From 1950 to 1955, under a five-year contract, the differentials narrowed because annual improvement increments and cost-of-living changes were given in flat absolute amounts, regardless of wage rates. With the contract of 1955, special adjustments were given to skilled workers to make up for the compression of the past five years and the annual improvement increments were henceforth expressed as percentages of wage rates rather than as flat amounts for all wage groups. The cost-of-living adjustments were still flat amounts and continue to be a narrowing factor.

Observing the wide swings in differentials it would appear that management has had no rigid principle on the matter. Even if it had preferences, their implementation would have been costly.

Summary

The periodic narrowing and widening of occupational differentials from 1858 to 1959 at the McCormick Works plus the data from three early government studies (Table D-2) implies that there has never been any long-run narrowing trend as this country matured industrially. Ober's 1907 wide occupational differential may, in the light of the McCormick Works data, have been the top of a wave rather than a half-way point on a long-run decline.

The influence of the cessation of immigration on differentials has been overestimated. In the 1920's common labor rates remained stable while skilled rates rose. At no time since the cessation of immigration have factory common labor rates risen due to a relative shortage of common labor. Our relatively slow pace of industrialization, plus immigration from more mature industrial countries, appears to have supplied this country with a near surplus of skilled workers from 1858 onward. This does not preclude temporary shortages during wartime nor brief shortages during the first part of a business pickup. After 1900 immigration from eastern and southern Europe depressed common labor rates until World War I. The wide occupational differentials which Ober found in 1907 appear to have been the temporary result of a combination of this flood of immigration and the wave of skilled worker unionism.

The Civil War and World War I at the McCormick Works narrowed differentials but not quite as expected. Following the first year of the Civil War, the net trend was toward widening due to skilled worker unionism and increasing skilled worker mobility. World War I had greater narrowing than the Civil War, at least if we begin it with 1916. In 1916 and 1919 strikes initiated by unskilled and semi-skilled labor in the twine and foundry departments were important forces in bringing about compression of differentials. Skilled labor mobility in World War I was substantially less than that of common labor. World War I, like the Civil War, was a tug of war between the forces which sought to widen and those which sought to narrow differentials. Common labor's higher mobility and leadership in unionization probably tipped the balance for wage differential compression during World War I. World War II found differentials widening from 153 to 170 and to a peak of 205 in 1945. Tight War Labor Board controls over common labor, Board concessions to skilled labor, separate craft union bargaining, and the compressed state of differentials at the start of the war are factors which helped produce the result. This widening of differentials during World War II was by no means limited to the Harvester Corporation, though it is not contended that such widening was general in manufacturing. Ober's study implies moderate narrowing but additional data are needed to learn how much of the narrowing occurred before, during, or after the war.

Contrary to current theory, the 100-year McCormick Works' evidence clearly indicates that prosperity widens and depression narrows occupational differentials. The reason for the widening in prosperity is perhaps because the business upturn begins with an accumulation of surplus unskilled workers and the preceding recession has interrupted the normal training of new skilled workers. The primary reason for the narrowing in depressions seems to have been a reluctance to cut wages of workers already at subsistence levels of income. In the last two recessions studied, 1921–1922 and 1929–1933, there was no narrowing (or widening) and common labor was cut proportionately.

Unionization has had a substantial effect on differentials, but whether it was to narrow, widen, or preserve the status quo depended on the nature of the union. The craft-structured Molders' Union, as early as the Civil War, tended to widen McCormick differentials. The industrially structured Knights of Labor which arose in 1886 substantially narrowed differentials. Machinists after 1900 had a widening influence. The strikes of unskilled workers in 1916 and 1919 narrowed differentials. The Farm Equipment Workers in the 1930's substantially narrowed differentials and the Pattern Makers spectacularly widened them during and after World War II. Today the differentials are carefully controlled by unions and management. The wide swings of the past will not be permitted.

The periodic rise and fall of differentials at the McCormick Works can be only partially explained by traditional labor market analysis. The fact seems to be that during most of its existence the McCormick Works had available to it ample supplies of both skilled and unskilled labor. Under these conditions occupational relationships were as much influenced by internal pressures (temporary and artificial shortages created by unions and management and worker notions of equity) as by external conditions of labor supply.

Because of its coverage of only one plant the McCormick Works experience should be primarily utilized to question existing theory rather than to draw firm conclusions. Neither should its implications be underestimated. This large manufacturing plant at the hub of our national transportation system could hardly have been very atypical of other metalworking and woodworking plants in Chicago or in other large northern cities.

Appendix E

A Summary View of the Status of Unionism at the McCormick Works

1858–1862   Pre-union.

1862–1886   Molders' Union conducted regular bargaining for the foundry. Very powerful though only admitted to membership 10 per cent of the work force. Conducted strikes in 1862, 1863, 1864, 1867, 1873, 1885, 1886.

1885–1886   Knights of Labor enrolled woodworkers and unskilled. Membership was about 60 per cent of work force. Co-operated with Molders during strike of 1886.

United Metalworkers enrolled skilled metal workers, conducted strikes in co-operation with Knights of Labor and Molders, 1886. Membership was about 25 per cent of work force.

The years 1885–1886 were crucial to the future of the unions. The unions won a violent plant-wide strike in 1885. A second, even more violent strike was won by the company in the spring of 1886, resulting in the end of collective bargaining relations with the company. A third short strike on May 1, 1886, resulted in the granting of the eight-hour day. The Haymarket bomb of May 4, 1886, and the subsequent trial, imprisonment, and execution of union leaders not only destroyed the leadership of the Metalworkers Union, but reinforced the resolve of the McCormick management (taken before the Haymarket riot) to operate non-union.

1887–1900   Non-union.

1900–1904   There was a revival of unionism after 1900, but actual bargaining and a signed contract were not achieved until 1903. Ten craft unions signed a contract for the three Chicago International Harvester plants after a strike in the Deering Works.

Estimated membership was 40 per cent of McCormick Works, but close to 100 per cent at Deering Works. In October, 1904, the company refused to renew the union agreement.

1904–1915   Non-union, repression of unions, combined with welfarism, stock gifts, profit sharing, sickness and accident insurance, pensions.

1916–1919   Prolonged, crippling strikes in 1916 and 1919, though unions were not recognized. Constant efforts made by the company to match union increases in other industries.

1920–1937   Non-union so far as effective collective bargaining was concerned, but in each International Harvester plant there was a company-dominated union known as a Works Council.

1935–1941   Active CIO organizing drives by both Farm Equipment Workers and the UAW in all International Harvester plants. Paid-up membership in these CIO unions was low except in five or six of the company's twenty plants, but sympathizers were many and the company's fear of the CIO gave these unions considerable upward wage pressure. Also a number of craft unions were recognized for some of the skilled employees.

1937–1941   Unaffiliated unions, former Works Councils, actually signed collective bargaining contracts. Most of them had well over 50 per cent of the employees as members.

1941–1960   Farm Equipment Workers were the bargaining agent for the McCormick Works until 1954 when the UAW became the bargaining agent. There was 100 per cent union membership. Strikes in this period occurred during 1941, 1946, 1948, 1950, 1952, 1953, 1958.

Bibliographical Note

The basic sources for this study have been the materials in the McCormick Collection of the State Historical Society Library, Madison, Wisconsin, and data made available by the International Harvester Company, Chicago, from its private files, and the George W. Perkins Papers, Butler Library, Columbia University. Material from the McCormick Collection included the original payroll books of the McCormick Harvesting Machine Company, 1849 and 1858–1902, of the International Harvester Company, 1902–1940, the Plano Company, 1882–1902, and the Deering Harvesting Machine Company, 1882–1896; also, the papers of the following individuals: Cyrus Hall McCormick (CHMcC I Papers in notes), Cyrus H. McCormick (CHMcC II Papers in notes), and Nettie Fowler McCormick (NFMcC Papers in notes) which include letters from Harold F. and Stanley R. McCormick (H.F.McC. and S.R.McC. in notes); and finally *The Journal and Convention Proceedings* of the International Union of Molders, Blacksmiths and Allied Workers, 1863–1886.

Secondary Sources:

Books

Bowen, William G. *Wage Behavior in the Post-War Period.* Princeton, N.J.: Princeton University Press, 1960.

Douglas, Paul H. *Real Wages in the United States, 1890–1926.* Boston: Houghton Mifflin Co., 1930.

———. *The Theory of Wages.* New York: The Macmillan Co., 1934.

Garraty, John A. *Right-Hand Man: The Life of George W. Perkins.* New York: Harper & Bros., 1960.

Hutchinson, William T. *Cyrus Hall McCormick.* 2 vols. New York: D. Appleton-Century Co., 1935.

Kaplan, A. D. H., Joel B. Derlam, and Robert F. Louzillotte. *Pricing in Big Business*. Washington, D.C.: The Brookings Institution, 1958.

Kendrick, John W. *Productivity Trends in the United States*. Princeton, N.J.: Princeton University Press, 1961.

Layer, Robert. *Earnings of Cotton Mill Operatives, 1825–1914*. Cambridge, Mass.: Harvard University Press, 1925.

Lebergott, Stanley. "Wage Trends, 1800–1900." In National Bureau of Economic Research. *Trends in the American Economy*. Princeton, N.J.: Princeton University Press, 1960.

Lewis, H. Gregg. *Unionism and Relative Wages in the United States*. Chicago: University of Chicago Press, 1963.

Long, Clarence D. *Wages and Earnings in the United States, 1860–1890*. Princeton, N.J.: Princeton University Press, 1960.

McKersie, Robert B. "Structural Factors and Negotiations in the I-H Co." In Arnold R. Webber, ed. *The Structure of Collective Bargaining*. Glencoe, Ill.: The Free Press, 1961.

National Industrial Conference Board. *The Economic Almanac, 1951–52*. New York: NICB, 1951.

Perry, George L. *Unemployment, Money Wage Rates, and Inflation*. Cambridge, Mass.: M.I.T. Press, 1966.

Rees, Albert. *The Economics of Trade Unions*. Chicago: The University of Chicago Press, 1962.

———. *New Measures of Wage-Earner Compensation in Manufacturing, 1914–57*. Occasional Paper 75. Washington, D.C.: National Bureau of Economic Research, Inc., 1960.

———. *Real Wages in Manufacturing, 1890–1914*. Princeton, N.J.: Princeton University Press, 1916.

Stigler, George J. *Capital and Rates of Return in Manufacturing Industries*. Princeton, N.J.: Princeton University Press, 1963.

Wright, David McCord. *The Impact of the Union*. New York: Harcourt Brace and Co., 1951.

Journal Articles

Eckstein, Otto and Thomas A. Wilson. "The Determination of Money Wages in American Industry." *Quarterly Journal of Economics*, 76 (Aug., 1962): 401.

Fogel, Walter. "Union Impact on Retail Food Wages in California." *Industrial Relations* (Univ. of Cal.), 6, No. 1 (Oct., 1966):79–94.

France, Robert R. "Wages, Unemployment, and Prices in the United States, 1890–1932, 1947–1957." *Industrial and Labor Relations Review*, 15 (Jan., 1962):171–90.

Hines, A. G. "Trade Unions and Wage Inflation in the U.K. 1893–1961." *Review of Economic Studies*, 31 (Oct., 1964):221–52.

Long, Clarence D. "The Illusion of Wage Rigidity." *Review of Economics and Statistics*, 42, No. 2, Part 1 (May, 1960):150–51.

Ozanne, Robert. "Union Impact: A Nineteenth-Century Case." *Industrial and Labor Relations Review*, 15 (April, 1962):350–75.
———. "Union Impact on Wage Levels and Income Distribution." *Quarterly Review of Economics*, 73 (May, 1959): 117–96.
Philips, A. W. "The Relation Between Unemployment and the Rate of Change of Money Wage Rates in the United Kingdom." *Economica*, N.S., 25 (Dec., 1958):283–99.
Rees, Albert. "Post-War Wage Determination in the Basic Steel Industry." *American Economic Review*, 41 (June, 1951), 389–464.

Government Documents

Aldrich, Nelson W. *Wholesale Prices, Wages and Transportation.* 52 Cong., 2 sess., Senate Report 1394, Pt. 1. Washington, March 3, 1893.
Bulletin of the Department of Labor, No. 18. Carroll D. Wright, ed. Washington, D.C.: GPO, 1898.
Economic Report of the President, 1962, 1963. Washington, D.C.: GPO, 1963, 1964.
Hearings Before the Joint Economic Committee of the Congress of the United States, 86 Cong., 2 sess., Part 2. *Historical and Comparative Rates of Production, Productivity, and Prices.* Washington, D.C.: GPO, 1959.
U.S. Bureau of the Census. *Historical Statistics, Colonial Times to 1957.* Washington, D.C.:GPO, 1960.
U.S. Bureau of Corporations. *Report on the International Harvester Company.* Washington, D.C.:GPO, 1913.
U.S. Department of Commerce. *Business Statistics.* Washington, D.C.: GPO, 1961.
U.S. Department of Labor, Bureau of Labor Statistics. *Handbook of Labor Statistics: 1950.* Bulletin No. 1016. Washington, D.C.: GPO, 1951.
U.S. vs. International Harvester Company and Others. Brief for the U.S. in District Court of the U.S. for District of Minnesota. October Term, 1913. McCormick Collection.
Weeks, Joseph D. "Report on the Statistics of Wages in the Manufacturing Industries with Supplementary Reports on the Average Retail Prices of Necessaries of Life and on Trade Societies, and Strikes and Lockouts." U.S. Bureau of the Census. *Report of the Census of 1880.* Washington, D.C.: GPO, 1881.

Newspapers

Chicago Times. 1800–1900.
Chicago Workingmen's Advocate. 1800–1900.

Notes

Chapter 1 • Introduction

1 Clarence D. Long, *Wages and Earnings in the United States, 1860–1890* (Princeton, N.J.: Princeton University Press, 1960); Albert Rees, *Real Wages in Manufacturing* (Princeton, N.J.: Princeton University Press, 1961); and Stanley Lebergott, "Wage Trends 1800–1900," in *NBER, Trends in the American Economy* (Princeton, N.J.: Princeton University Press, 1960), pp. 449–502.

2 Paul Douglas, *Real Wages in the United States, 1891–1926* (Boston: Houghton Mifflin, 1930) and Douglas, *The Theory of Wages* (New York: Macmillan Co., 1934).

3 A. W. Philips, "The Relation Between Unemployment and the Rate of Change of Money Wage Rates in the United Kingdom, 1861–1957," *Economica*, N.S. 25 (Dec., 1958):903–20.

4 Ibid.

5 Hearings Before the Joint Economics Committee of Congress of the U.S., 86 Cong., 1 sess., Part 2, *Historical and Comparative Rates of Production, Productivity, and Prices* (1959), p. 398.

6 Otto Eckstein and Thomas A. Wilson, "The Determination of Money Wages in American Industry," *Quarterly Journal of Economics*, 76 (Aug., 1962):401.

7 John W. Kendrick, *Productivity Trends in the United States* (Princeton, N.J.: Princeton University Press, 1961), p. 197.

8 Ibid., p. 196.

9 Albert Rees, "Postwar Wage Determination in the Basic Steel Industry," *American Economic Review*, 41 (June, 1951):389–464.

10 Robert Ozanne, "Impact of Unions on Wage Levels and Income Distribution," *Quarterly Journal of Economics*, 73 (May, 1959):177–96.

Chapter 2 • Wage Profiles

1 A portion of this chapter has appeared as Robert Ozanne, "Union Impact: A Nineteenth-Century Case," *Industrial and Labor Relations Review*, 15 (April, 1962):350–75. It is reproduced here with the permission of the *ILRR Review*.

2 For year-to-year comparisons of average wage rates, the first payroll period (about the first week in April) for each year was judged to be superior to yearly average hourly earnings. This is because the April figure always fell within the seasonal period of peak production while annual averages would show lower piece rate earnings due to their decline in the dull late summer and fall seasons. Annual day rate earnings would average higher than the April figures because in slack seasons there would be included a smaller proportion of unskilled workers. Since the length of the slack seasons varied considerably from year to year, the annual data are not measuring the same thing from year to year; however, from 1915 to 1924, when April wages were not available, annual averages were used in the profiles and charts.

3 Nelson W. Aldrich, *Wholesale Prices, Wages and Transportation* (52 Cong., 2 sess., Senate Report 1394, pt. 2, Washington, March 3, 1893). Aldrich was Chairman of the Senate Committee on Finance and the document is known also as the Aldrich Report.

4 *Chicago Times*, 1867: May 4, p. 8; May 6, p. 4.

5 *Chicago Workingmen's Advocate*, May 25, 1875.

6 Letters to McCormick agents, L.P.C. [Letter Press Copybook]. McC.H.M.Co., Aug. 4, 1873.

7 C. A. Spring to Cyrus H. McCormick, L.P.C., McC.H.M.Co., Sept. 6, 1873.

8 Employment data from Payroll Books, McC.H.M.Co.; profits from letter, C. A. Spring to C.H.McC. I, Sept. 1, 1871, CHMcC I Papers; letter, Frank H. Mathews to idem, Sept. 22, 1874, CHMcC I Papers; letter, Frank H. Mathews to idem, Oct. 4, 1875, CHMcC I Papers; Wm. T. Hutchinson, *Cyrus Hall McCormick*, 2 vols. (New York: D. Appleton-Century Co., 1935), II:607, 117 (for 1877, 1878, 1879).

9 Letters, Frank H. Mathews to C.H.McC. I, Sept. 22, 1874 and August 11, 1875, CHMcC I Papers; letter, C. A. Spring to idem, Sept. 27, 1881, CHMcC I Papers, Subject Files, Series 2A, Box 53.

10 Monthly Report of Local 23 and Local 233, *Iron Molders Journal*, 1873–1879, Library of the State Historical Society, Madison, Wisconsin.

11 Monthly Report of Local 233, *Iron Molders Journal*, May, 1881; C.H.McC. II Diary, 1882:Jan. 12, April 3.

12 Letter, C.H.McC. II to N.F.McC., April 13, 1885, NFMcC Papers, Subject File Series 3B, Box 5.

13 Payroll Books, Deering Harvester Machine Company.

14 Payroll Books, Plano Harvesting Machine Company.

15 N.F.McC. to E. K. Butler and C. H. Spring, Oct. 30, 1887, NFMcC Papers.

16 N.F.McC. to E. K. Butler, July 8, 1894, NFMcC Papers.

17 H.F.McC. to C.H.McC. II, March 24, 1900, McC.H.M.Co. LPC, p. 267.

18 S.R.McC. to C.H.McC. II, Dec., 1903, CHMcC II Papers, Private File No. 0–20.

19 See the E.A.S. Clarke Report, E. A. S. Clarke to C.H.McC. II, Aug. 19, 1904, CHMcC II Papers.

20 U.S. Bureau of the Census, *Historical Statistics, Colonial Times to 1957* (Washington, D.C.: GPO, 1960), 73.

21 Paul H. Douglas, *Real Wages in the United States, 1890–1926* (Boston: Houghton Mifflin Company, 1930), p. 96.

22 U.S. Bureau of Corporations, *Report on the International Harvester Company* (Washington, D.C.: GPO, 1913), p. 234.

23 1910 Wage Resolution, Jan., 1910, CHMcC II Papers, P–20.

24 C.H.McC. II to H.F.McC., Sept. 27, 1916, CHMcC II Papers, Private File Drawer 114, No. 2.

25 Ibid., Sept. 10, 1917.

26 Ibid., Oct. 9, 1917, and March 19, 1918.

27 Ibid., Feb. 18, 1920.

28 Real wage changes calculated from data compiled by Clarence D. Long in "The Illusion of Wage Rigidity," *Review of Economics and Statistics* 42, No. 2, Pt. 1 (May, 1960): 150–51.

29 Rees, "Post War Wage Determination in the Basic Steel Industry," *American Economic Review*, 41 (June, 1951): 398–404.

30 Ibid., p. 396.

31 See George W. Perkins to C.H.McC. II, May 4, 1916, Box 23, George W. Perkins Collection, Butler Library, Columbia University.

32 Works Managers Meetings, Dec. 27 and 29, 1920, I.H.Co. Files, Chicago.

33 Ibid., 1922: May 16, 17, and 27.

34 Ibid., May 27, 1923; and McCormick Payroll Books, McCormick Collection.

35 Works Managers Meeting, Oct. 23, 1922, I.H.Co. Files, Chicago.

36 Ibid., 1922: Dec. 18; 1923: Jan. 3, 9, 12.

37 Ibid., 1923: April 9, 16, 27, May 28.

38 Ibid., June 4, 1923.

39 John W. Kendrick, *Productivity Trends in the United States* (Princeton, N.J.: Princeton University Press, 1961), p. 465.

40 Works Managers Meetings, 1923: July 6, Oct. 22; 1924: Feb. 22, July 7, I.H.Co. Files, Chicago.

41 Ibid., July 7, 1924.

42 Ibid., Dec. 6, 1926.

43 Ibid., 1924: Feb. 11; 1925: Oct. 19, Dec. 7; 1926: April 26, June 21, Dec. 6; 1927: March 8, May 16; 1928: April 23; 1929: Feb. 25, Sept. 9, Dec. 30.

44 McCormick Works Payroll Books, McCormick Collection.
45 Ibid.

Chapter 3 • Wage Movements for Three Competitive Agricultural Implement Companies, 1888–1902

1 Molders' Union records, reports of Local 233, Library, State Historical Society, Madison, Wisconsin.

Chapter 4 • The Wage Impact of Trade Unionism

1 See the companion volume to this study, Robert Ozanne, *A Century of Labor Management Relations* (Madison, Wis.: University of Wisconsin Press, 1967).
2 For a fuller treatment of the material in this paragraph and the preceding one, see ibid., pp. 240–41.
3 Works Managers Meeting, October 11, 1926, I.H.Co. file, Chicago.

Chapter 5 • The Wage Impact of Market Demand for Labor

1 William G. Bowen, *Wage Behavior in the Post-War Period* (Princeton, N.J.: Princeton University Press, 1960), p. 16.
2 U.S. Department of Labor, Bureau of Labor Statistics, *Handbook of Labor Statistics: 1950*, Bulletin No. 1016 (Washington, D.C.: GPO, 1951), p. 142.
3 The indicators of economic downturn here are those of the National Bureau of Economic Research as reprinted in Hearings Before the Joint Economics Committee of the Congress of the U.S., 86 Cong., 1 sess. Part 2, *Historical and Comparative Rates of Production, Productivity, and Prices* (1959), p. 398.
  The financial condition of the Harvester firm in these recessions can be seen in Table 27, Chapter 7.
4 Paul Douglas, *Real Wages in the United States 1890–1926* (Boston: Houghton Mifflin, 1930), p. 96.
5 Robert Layer, *Earnings of Cotton Mill Operatives, 1825–1914* (Cambridge, Mass.: Harvard University Press, 1925), p. 23.
6 Ibid., pp. 36–37.
7 Albert Rees, *The Economics of Trade Unions* (Chicago, Ill.: University of Chicago Press, 1962), p. 79.
8 Ibid.
9 H. Gregg Lewis, *Unionism and Relative Wages in the United States* (Chicago, Ill.: University of Chicago Press, 1963), pp. 193–94.
10 Milton Friedman, "Some Comments on the Significance of Labor Unions for Economic Policy," in David McCord Wright, *The Impact of the Union* (New York: Harcourt, Brace and Company, 1951), pp. 226–31.
11 Interview with Wm. Reilly, Manager, Labor Relations, May 27, 1964.
12 International Harvester Labor Market Summaries, 1945–49, Office Memo, I.H.Co. files, Chicago.

Chapter 6 • The Wage Impact of Value Productivity

1 Paul Douglas, *Real Wages in the United States, 1890–1926* (Boston: Houghton Mifflin, 1930) and *The Theory of Wages* (New York: Macmillan Co., 1934).

2 Albert Rees, *Real Wages in Manufacturing, 1890–1914* (Princeton, N.J.: Princeton University Press, 1961), p. 123.

3 Fabricant in Hearings Before the Joint Economic Committee of the Congress of the U.S., 86 Cong., 1 sess., Part 2, *Historical and Comparative Rates of Production, Productivity, and Prices* (1959), pp. 319–20.

4 The data for this calculation on productivity are from John W. Kendrick, *Productivity Trends in the United States* (Princeton, N.J.: Princeton University Press, 1961), pp. 328–30, Col. 5. For the wage data see Sources for Table 1.

5 Ibid., pp. 124–27.

6 Ibid., p. 198.

7 Ibid., Table 33, p. 129.

Chapter 7 • The Wage Impact of the Product Market

1 U.S. v. International Harvester Company and others, Brief for the U.S. in District Court of the U.S. for District of Minnesota, October Term, 1913, p. 62, on file in the McCormick Collection.

2 George J. Stigler, *Capital and Rates of Return in Manufacturing Industries* (Princeton, N.J.: Princeton University Press, 1963), pp. 213–15. In a listing of the percentage of shipments in dollars contributed by the four largest firms, Stigler puts agricultural implements at 72.4 per cent in 1935, 49.5 per cent in 1947, and 55.2 per cent in 1954. This compares with 85 per cent by one firm, International Harvester, in 1902.

3 George W. Perkins to William E. Corey, Oct. 4, 1909. George W. Perkins papers, Butler Library, Columbia University.

4 John A. Garraty, *Right-Hand Man* (New York: Harper, 1960), pp. 114–15; and George W. Perkins to J. P. Morgan, Nov. 11, 1909, GWP papers.

5 Perkins to J. P. Morgan, July 23, 1907, ibid.

Chapter 8 • Summary of Findings

1 Robert Ozanne, "Union Impact on Wage Levels and Income Distribution," *Quarterly Review of Economics*, 73, No. 2 (May, 1959): 177–96.

2 Walter Fogel, "Union Impact on Retail Food Wages in California," *Industrial Relations* (Univ. of Cal.) 6, No. 1 (Oct., 1966): 79–94.

Appendix D • A Century of Occupational Differentials in Manufacturing

1 Appendix D first appeared in the *Review of Economics and Statistics*, 44, No. 3 (Aug., 1962): 292–99, and is reprinted here by permission of the editor.

2 See Harry Ober, "Occupational Wage Differentials, 1907–1947," *Monthly Labor Review*, 67 (July, 1948), 127–34. Ober did provide continuous annual occupational differentials based on big city union scales for building trades and skilled common labor. It is a mistake, however, to assume that manufacturing differentials followed building trades differentials or that the same causes affected both.

3 M. W. Reder, "The Theory of Occupation Wage Differentials," *American Economic Review*, 45 (Dec., 1955): 846–48.

4 H. M. Douty, "Union Impact on Wage Structures," *Proceedings of the Sixth Annual Meeting, Industrial Relations Research Association* (1953), p. 67.

5 Correspondence, CHMcC I Papers, 1863, 1864, McCormick Collection, Library of the State Historical Society, Madison, Wis.

6 *Chicago Tribune*, April 28, 1916, p. 3.

7 Ibid., July 16, 1919, p. 7.

8 B.L.S. Wage Chronologies for Ford Motor Co. No. 99; General Motors, Series 4, No. 9; United States Steel Corporation, No. 106.

9 Clark Kerr, "Market and Power Forces," in John Dunlop, *Theory of Wage Determination* (New York: Macmillan Co., 1957), p. 189, *n.* 1.

10 Lloyd Reynolds and Cynthia Taft, *The Evolution of Wage Structure* (New Haven, Conn.: Yale University Press, 1956), p. 363.

Index

Across-the-board increases. *See* Raises, general
Adamson Eight-Hour Act, 39, 44
AHE. *See* Average hourly earnings
Aldrich, Nelson W., 20–21
American Federation of Labor, 41, 56
Anarchism, 26
Annual wage increase, 76, 125
Anti-unionism. *See* Avoidance of unions
Apprentices, 151
Automation. *See* Mechanization
Average hourly earnings: historical studies of, 3–4; McCormick Works compared to U.S. manufacturing, 4, 34; varies with time period, 11–12; as used in wage profiles, 14; as used in plant average wage, 14; in 1874, 25; during World War I, 38; for unskilled workers, 63; 1860 compared to 1960, 70; and employment changes, 83–88 *passim*; in depressions, 93; effect of unions on, 102, 124, 125; effect of productivity on, 109, 126; and labor costs, 111–12; relationship to profits, 118
Avoidance of unions: and the McCormick family, 33, 121; responsible for wage increases, 34–36, 37, 44, 54–55, 64, 73–74, 75–76, 94, 119, 121; at United States Steel Corporation, 43; cost of, 58; at Plano Works, 64–65;

depresses wages, 65, 124; destroyed unions, 65, 124; at Wisconsin Steel Works, 74; employers' associations, 96–97; use of lockouts, 97; and product market, 120; and public opinion, 121

Bargaining, collective. *See* Collective bargaining
Bonuses, 38
Bowen, William, 83–84
Boycott, 115
Brooks, R. G., 34
Butler, E. K., 33

Chicago Malleable Iron Company, 26, 29
Chicago Metal Trades Association, 47, 51. *See also* Employers' Associations
Chicago Metal Workers Union, 61
Chicago Southwest Side Employers, 96. *See also* Employers' Associations
Chrysler Corporation, 103
CIO. *See* Congress of Industrial Organizations
City-town wage differential. *See* Differential, wage
Civil War. *See* Wars — Civil War
Clarke, E. A. S., 36
Clayton Anti-Trust Act, 44
Collective bargaining: used by skilled